UNTIL
SHILOH
COMES

UNTIL SHILOH COMES

TESTIMONY OF A LIVING GOD

SOPHIA ROSE

This is a work of nonfiction. Some names have
been changed to protect privacy.

Cover and design: Travis Hasenour

ISBN 979-8-9908512-3-8

www.untilshilohcomes.com

Thank you for setting me free

CHAPTER
ONE

The day after my youngest child died, friends stopped by, insisting I go to their house for the evening. As I followed them across the street from their car, I stopped, stunned. I recognized nothing—not their house, not the streetlights, not even the street, though I had been there dozens of times.

"This changes everything," I whispered. It was not the world that had changed, but me.

For years, I thought Ben's death was the defining event of my life. But I was wrong.

The real shift, the point around which the entirety of my life pivots, happened on a day that I did not record in my diary. I do not recall if it was a Tuesday or a Wednesday. I only remember the moment itself which stands out in my memory clearly, a gift to the part of me that marvels at miracles.

I had been living in Egypt for six months when it happened.

One late afternoon, I walked alone along the sea, pausing at a point of land that jutted into the water. The illusion of being surrounded by water created a strange feeling of detachment. A deep clarity descended, of a kind that happens only rarely. Suddenly, I was fully aware of my life. I saw myself as though from a great distance. And I was totally lost. All that I had done in my life to find meaning and happiness had been wholly ineffective.

I stared over the Gulf of Aqaba. I hadn't a single idea what to do. No next step. No plan. Oddly, the realization of utter helplessness ushered in a serene acceptance. Then, I felt something in my chest. Something so strong that it could not be quashed. I spontaneously whispered a passionate plea to whoever or whatever might be in charge.

"Please, I need a spiritual guide."

Peace followed that whisper.

The quiet moment was broken, then, by a bitter thought. *Too bad I wouldn't trust anyone.*

Those close to me, those I trusted, always ended up hurting me. I was not willing to seek guidance from yet another person who would betray me in some new and unavoidable way. I was too wise, I thought, to let that happen again.

I turned from the sea and, under the darkening sky, walked back to my apartment, doing what I was good at—carrying on. I never imagined, not even for an instant, that I would receive an answer.

CHAPTER
TWO

In the small town on the Sinai Peninsula where I was living, I discovered a Malaysian restaurant. The first time I dined there, the young owner took my order and served it himself. It was early in the season yet, and few tourists were around so he sat next to me, telling me some of the challenges he had experienced in his young life and what had led him to open his restaurant.

Hisham was intelligent and ambitious with an engaging smile, and that evening I agreed to tutor him in English in exchange for meals at his restaurant.

One week after the plea into the sea, I saw Hisham. He had come to my table with a big smile, greatly excited. As I ate, he sat next to me, animatedly telling me of the Scottish healer

Shiloh Kairos he had met. He described the healing session they had, repeating over and over how much it had helped him. Hisham enthused, nearly breathless, about Shiloh's abilities. He badly wanted to give me his contact information.

But I refused to ask for it. I had met plenty of healers in my years of searching for truth. I was universally disillusioned by ineptness or egoistic behavior or a lack of depth. I have no doubt that some people know some things, but then they overreached, advising others far beyond the appropriate level of their insight. I had been burned by their ill-placed self-confidence more times than I cared to admit. In any case, if my son's death was the reward for my extensive efforts to understand life, then I was finished.

I resisted Hisham's multiple attempts to arrange a meeting with Shiloh. A week later, however, when he organized an evening of meditation at his house, I went. He seemed so proud of the renovation of his rooftop deck, and it was embarrassing to consistently decline his kind invitations.

When I arrived at Hisham's house, Shiloh was the only other person there. He greeted me, his manner quiet yet attentive. Relaxed and unpretentious, he did not seek to impress me with a litany of his spiritual experiences, which I greatly appreciated.

After tea, we went to the rooftop, which was indeed quite lovely. Hisham lit a small brazier and we sat on cushions.

We didn't meditate. Instead, we talked, and when I left at the end of the evening, I recall thinking that Shiloh was a kind person though somewhat enigmatic. It didn't occur to me to ask for his spiritual advice. Many times I had been naive enough to trust others, and I was determined not to be foolish again.

Over the next few days, I saw Shiloh at the vegan restaurant on the beach. I saw him as I walked to the market, and then, later along the sea. Each time I bumped into him, he was kind and soft-spoken and in no hurry to go elsewhere. I found myself wondering why he was talking to me. He seemed to want nothing. Not mothering, nor attention, nor relationship, nor even a sympathetic ear. I had never met anyone so self-contained. Most people want something from me and are often willing to manipulate me, either through charm or deception, to get it. But he displayed none of the self-seeking behavior I was familiar with.

Finally, it happened. The thing that broke through my defenses.

I was sitting on the beach when Shiloh walked by, and seeing me, stopped. He sat on a rock a few feet away, giving me space yet remaining close enough for conversation. I asked him about his plans for the day and he inquired about my work. Then, together we looked out over the sea at the waves crashing on the reef in the distance.

The sun was quite warm and, eventually, Shiloh stood and dove into the shallow water to cool off. Although I was wearing my swimsuit beneath my clothes, I was reluctant to undress. Not in front of Shiloh and certainly not in front of the two Egyptian men who were swimming nearby.

After Shiloh finished his dip in the water, he returned to his stone, where he settled once again. After several minutes, he looked over at me and then away. Then, gently, he said, "You have a problem with body image, and it really holds you back." It was neither a question nor an accusation, but a mildly-stated observation.

I froze. I was certain I had displayed no sign of how badly I wanted to go in the water nor of the battle that raged inside me preventing me from doing so. But somehow Shiloh knew the agony that paralyzed me.

I remained awkwardly quiet, unwilling to acknowledge the truth of his statement.

We sat for a while longer until I excused myself to finish some work. In my room I sat on the bed and stared into the mirror at the normal-sized person who felt like an elephant. I cried for a long time. Something was very wrong with me, and I didn't know what it was.

The next morning, I texted Shiloh and asked if he had time for a healing session.

Later that afternoon, Shiloh met me at a beach cafe and we sat at a table in the sand. Relieving me of the burden of forming a question, he began to speak.

Without preliminary, he went straight to the heart of my most serious issue. In my effort to protect myself from being hurt, he explained, because of all that I had been through, I had shut down completely. He told me that he could see a representation of this as a sort of hood over my head. But in shutting down, I was cutting myself off from God and from my own intuition.

His accuracy stunned me. I had not told Shiloh of my youngest son's death and the bitterness that had caused me to abandon spirituality. Further, I had not spoken of other serious blows in my life—the long estrangement from my mother and the death of my sister who had been a motherly proxy. I had not mentioned the two marriages, so deeply traumatic that I had refused to consider the possibility of another relationship. I certainly had not told him that as a young child, I had been molested for several years by a relative. We had only spoken of the most superficial aspects of my life and how I had recently moved to this small village to restart my freelance writing career. Yet, somehow, he had seen beyond my cheerful exterior, beyond the friendly confidence plastered over the darkness.

At his words, it was as though a huge bandage that I had placed over my heart dissolved and every painful feeling I had been suppressing for a lifetime came flying out. I cried until I couldn't hear Shiloh. I cried so much I couldn't see.

Finally, I recovered enough to carefully consider his words. My reasons for mistrusting others were quite sound, I thought. How should I have responded to all that had happened to me? I reflected on the mistreatment, accumulated over a lifetime.

"Everyone I have ever known has betrayed me. Horribly," I said defensively. "Why *should* I trust anyone?"

Shiloh responded calmly. He wasn't asking me to trust anyone, he said. People act out of their own pain and most have a great deal of it.

I relaxed, relieved. He knew that people were likely to hurt me, over and over again, exactly as had been my experience. Then he said that which I most needed to hear.

"God is always there for you. Always. He has never betrayed you."

I said nothing. I wasn't sure there was a god who took notice of me.

Perhaps he saw my unspoken skepticism because Shiloh went on. If I were to ask for a sign that God is near, that He hears me, he said, then I would receive it.

I struggled to believe him. "Really?"

His voice carried the weight of total conviction. "One hundred percent."

I marveled at how he could be so sure. Shiloh clearly was a man who felt God as a very real force in his life. Of course, I thought, God would speak to such a devout man. But I had abandoned all semblance of my spiritual self after Ben's suicide three years earlier. The only good feeling I had ever had about myself, amid the childhood abuse, two failed marriages, and familial estrangement was that despite all I had been through, I was a good mother. Then that was taken from me.

I have no memory of the other things that Shiloh said to me that day. I had been holding in pain for so long that simply being able to cry was a gift.

CHAPTER
THREE

The next day I sat on the beach on the north end of town, far from the busy cafes, waiting for the man with the camel to leave. The camel had a long gaping gash on its hind leg, and the man was trying to force it to sit in the water. The camel made terrible braying noises, protesting every tug, and resisting every push. Eventually, the man gave up and scooped seawater with his hands in a great arc toward the gash in the camel's haunch. The camel brayed again, this time in pain.

As I watched the cleansing ritual, I considered Shiloh's words from the day before. If I wished proof that God was near, that I was not completely alone, all I had to do was ask for a sign.

I wasn't sure the God that Shiloh referred to had any use for me, having ignored Him for so many years.

After the man led his now-quiet camel away, I crept out into the clear sea. The water was barely chest high, and I crouched until I was submerged to my neck. Still raw and bruised from the prior day's epic tears, I tried to relax into the salty water.

The lifelessness of the clear water was remarkable. For months, I had visited the edge of the sea each afternoon but had not seen the signs of life typical of natural waters. Nearly eerie was the absence of shells, seaweed, and even fish.

I bobbed back and forth in the waves, deeply frightened that I wasn't worthy enough to receive the attention of God, despite Shiloh's assurance. Finally, after several minutes, I summoned sufficient courage to risk what could turn out to be a devastating blow in an already disappointing life. In a little whisper, I said, "Shiloh said You would show Yourself if I called. So, I am calling." If anyone were listening, they would know what I meant.

I opened my eyes. I had just started to wonder how long it might be before I received a response when I spied something strange in the water in the distance. I squinted to see it better. A swiftly moving ripple from the direction of the reef. It was heading rapidly for me, straight as a loosed arrow.

The movement stopped in the clear water no more than

eighteen inches from my nose. An eel. Staring right at me. I returned its stare, in total shock.

I don't know what I expected. A voice from the sky? A parting of the clouds? But this was perfect. If there was a God of all creation then He would certainly use nature to communicate.

I held its gaze, breathless, for nearly a minute, the only movement a fine rippling of the long fin along the eel's back as it maintained its place in the water, looking me in the eyes. Then I shifted in my half-crouched position searching for a firmer grip on the sand beneath me. That broke the spell. The eel turned and swam slowly away. I watched it go, completely dumbfounded.

I was not alone after all.

CHAPTER
FOUR

On its own, an eel randomly showing up to stare at me would have been amazing. But the creature had raced to me and placed itself directly in front of my face seconds after I had asked, begged actually, for God to send a sign that He heard me. It was beyond what my rational mind could attribute to chance.

In that moment, I believed. That conscious decision to believe that the eel was a message from God represented a great healing. I had been determined for years to shut everyone and everything out of my life. But Shiloh had lifted me into a place of hope, opening me to the possibility of God's presence in my life. The eel's arrival was the first miracle that I experienced after meeting Shiloh. It was not the last.

I had already seen that Shiloh seemed to know things about me—deeply personal things that no one knew. When I invited him for dinner a few days later, I was to discover this was not unusual.

After enjoying a vegetable stir fry, we sat on the couch drinking tea. At one point, he straightened, quite abruptly as though startled, before relaxing again completely.

"What happened?" I asked.

Your roommate is here, he said.

I had not heard the opening or closing of the large metal gate leading from the street into the courtyard. Nor had there been any other sound to indicate that someone was on their way up the stairs to our apartment.

"How do you know?" I asked, bewildered.

He responded that God often lets him know before people arrive.

At that moment, my roommate entered. She declined my offer of a meal and, instead, joined me on the couch. She and Shiloh, who had met briefly while on the main street a few days earlier, began an earnest discussion of a topic that I don't recall but didn't include me. After a few minutes of listening from the edge of their conversation, I went into the kitchen and began to wash the dishes. The awkwardness I felt was a holdover from a childhood in which I felt quite acutely the invisibility of being in the middle of thirteen siblings. I told myself that my self-worth was not related to being included in a conversation, and I focused on cleaning.

After my roommate left to go to her room and music began to float through her closed door, Shiloh turned to where I had settled on the couch with another cup of tea.

"I'm sorry it seemed as though I was ignoring you. I needed to focus on her because God asked me to be careful."

Remarkably, he had known exactly how I had been feeling though I was absolutely sure I had displayed no sign of discomfort. More than that, it was apparent that he was guided in all his interactions in a way that was quite specific and compassionate.

That evening Shiloh and I spoke of Ben. Rather, we spoke of my response to Ben's death, which seemed as fresh to me as when it had happened three years earlier. He listened to my outpouring of sorrow and then spoke for a long time about the eternal and sacred path of each soul. Then he told me that my seemingly endless pain arose not as much from sorrow as from guilt. He assured me that my grief would abate when I realized I was not responsible for the choices made by my son's soul.

A part of me was sure that if Shiloh knew the whole story, he might not say this. I was sure that had I been a better mother, then my son would now be alive. It was a theme we would return to several times in the coming years.

Eventually, in his care, I would release all of the pain and be left with nothing but deep gratitude for the beautiful soul that was Ben. But all that was to come. I did not know then how deeply Shiloh understood my pain or how willing he was to help me through the morass left by this and other traumas.

That evening I witnessed the depth of the guidance that he received, and I knew for certain that he operated on a quite different level of awareness. With his permission, from then onward my role shifted from that of healing client to student. We met many evenings, talking until late in a nearby cafe.

CHAPTER
FIVE

Whenever Shiloh and I spoke, he told me of God, God's love, God's mystery, and the way to hold a sacred space for God in my life. He told me, too, of his remarkable life, his deep spiritual journey, and some of the great suffering he had experienced on his path to God. I soaked up the faith that he radiated, quiet faith, that did not boast but was evident in every action and every word. Despite being raised in a religious home in the Bible Belt, I hadn't known anyone like him.

One afternoon, as we sat on a log near the sea, he shared a low-sugar dessert that he had purchased from a nearby cafe. When he got up to offer me a portion, he stumbled slightly and scraped his leg against the log, removing a patch of skin. After he placed a portion of the dessert on my plate, he sat back down. He pointed to the raw skin on his leg, and wondered aloud what it was about.

"How do you know it is about something?" I asked.

Everything that happens to us, big or small, is arranged by God for us, he said. Even this bee has a message. He pointed to the small winged creature that had landed on his foot.

Years later I would recall that conversation and see the truth of his words. But on that day, I wasn't sure what to make of it. How could a bee bring a message? I didn't contradict him. I didn't ask about the message borne by the bee. I put his comment in a compartment in my mind. I had a lot of things in there—things that I didn't understand, but was willing to consider because of who he had shown himself to be.

One day, as we sat sipping sweet Bedouin tea at one of the many cafes along the shore, I was feeling slightly anxious because I had a question for Shiloh and I was uncertain of his reply. I wished to visit St Catherine's Monastery, the oldest continuously occupied monastery in the world. I was not sure Shiloh would wish to go with me. Despite my reluctance to ask for companionship, even less did I relish the thought of hiring a taxi to drive me alone one and a half hours into the desert. Finally, I overcame the fear of being turned down.

"Shiloh, I was thinking of going to St Catherine's monastery. Are you at all interested?"

Shiloh looked at me, his expression radiant. His happiness surprised me because he did not tend to have strong reactions. Then he told me that he had asked God to arrange a trip to St Catherine's if it was His will.

Apparently, it was meant to be.

A few days later, we were seated in the back of a comfortable sedan on the way to the monastery. I had something else to ask Shiloh. I had offered him payment for that first healing session, as was my habit with other spiritual teachers. But he had given me much advice over the past weeks and had asked for nothing. I did not wish to take advantage of his generosity.

When I finally broached the subject of money, a topic I found difficult to speak of, Shiloh quickly put me at ease. He told me that he asks for no payment for any of his healing work.

"What if you need money?" I couldn't quite grasp what he was saying.

"If I need anything," he said, "I ask if God will provide it. God provides me with whatever I need. Not necessarily from the person I have helped but sometimes later in a different way. God always finds a way to give us what we need."

I considered this astonishing statement for a while. Then, I told him that I was uncomfortable with not offering something to him for his guidance. Shiloh said that any donation in exchange for his teaching was a topic that I should address with God.

My estimation of Shiloh's integrity, already high, ballooned. Many people seem willing to speak of God and pray and do charitable works. Even people who pledge to God as religious persons are often provided support from their church. I hadn't known anyone willing to completely grant to God their very subsistence on this Earth.

When Shiloh spoke of faith and of placing God first, it was not talk. Shiloh put all aspects of his life fully in God's hands.

CHAPTER
SIX

For a little over two months that spring, Shiloh provided intensive instruction in living a life of faith. It is difficult to summarize all that he taught me. All that he did showed me what faith looked like. All that he spoke of was from a perspective of faith in God's plan for each of us.

Shiloh spent much time explaining that I must delve into my deepest self and root out with love the beliefs I held about myself and the world. Only then could I see the truth of everything, particularly myself. He taught me how to do this but all that he spoke of is impossible to repeat here; it could fill several books. I listened carefully, but it would take more than a few weeks for me to abandon the ingrained perspectives of pain and distrust.

In those two months, however, he planted a massive number of seeds in my consciousness, seeds of living a life of faith. When one of those seeds germinated, sometimes months or even years later, the moment that it burst felt like a grand "aha!" It would have been easy for me to think that the understanding sprang from myself. But I could see how he cultivated the entire process of my stepwise growth and that my life's experiences were needed to water those seeds so they could germinate and grow.

Over the next several years, whenever one of those seeds yielded a bloom, I would think back to Egypt when he first told me all that I needed to know. The gradual integration of what he taught was a beautiful, unfolding process.

My life, however, had been quite troubled. I had many hab-its to release and a vast amount of unprocessed emotions and experiences to sift through. My difficulty lay, not in a conscious wish to remain a distrustful person but in not see-ing the ways that I attempted to protect myself from life. Those habits, Shiloh explained, kept me from seeing life as it truly was and prevented me from experiencing God's perfect love for me.

I could not consciously will myself to trust, as much as I

wanted to. I could not see those shackles of beliefs and per-
sonality that I had developed in response to the world, even
when I labored hard to do so. Shiloh could. He saw clearly
all that blocked me. His patience with me and the gradual
process was incredible. Even now, looking back at all I went
through, my overriding impression is wonder that Shiloh
had the patience to see me through it.

I was not an apt student. Over the next few years, I was
to become incredibly frustrated with myself for my slowness
to understand and incorporate into my life the concepts he
had given me in Egypt. My inability to see the ways my ego
fooled me and my lack of focus were unacceptable to me.
But Shiloh accepted all of my frustratingly slow progress
with calmness and non-judgment. His patience was a lesson
in how I should treat myself.

CHAPTER
SEVEN

In my 30's, in my desperation to overcome my difficult childhood and traumatic first marriage, I saw a psycho-therapist twice a week. Eventually, I began to suspect that the therapist was not helping me but when I spoke of leaving therapy, he insisted that any desire I had to end therapy with him was not healthy. He thought he was helping me by advising me to stay in a therapeutic relationship that had long since run its course. Finally, in an immense effort of self-preservation, I broke free. But I had floundered along for nearly ten years listening to a man who not only did not help me, but insisted that my correct feelings were, in fact, a sign of illness. A few years later, after my second troubled marriage, I saw another therapist. She was somewhat helpful, mostly in helping me to identify my emotions, some-thing I should have learned as a child. Despite learning to acknowledge my feelings, however, the core reasons for my difficulties in life, those that led me to establish relationships with deeply troubled men, remained wholly unaddressed. After nearly 15 years in formal therapy, I still carried the symptoms of childhood trauma, meaninglessness, and lack of self-worth. That I even spoke to Shiloh was a sort of mir-acle in itself.

In the two months I had known him, Shiloh had done more for me than the extensive psychotherapy I had gone through. Shiloh gave me a blueprint for self-love and trust in God. With it came new hope that there was meaning to my life, meaning beyond work and beyond collecting friends, and more purposeful than seeking interesting experiences. I soaked up his guidance, yearning for the peace that he embodied.

When it was time to leave Egypt to celebrate my son's grad-uation from college, I knew it was unlikely that I would return. Despite its attractiveness as a place to live comfort-ably for relatively low cost, Egypt had been difficult. Not because of a language barrier—enough people spoke English that I could get along easily. It was the constant need to assert myself. Egypt offered the perfect opportunity to learn to set boundaries, Shiloh pointed out.

He was right. At one point, my landlord tried to evict me from my apartment, I assume because she had found someone who would pay more. I was already intending to move to a different apartment for my own reasons, but this sudden, difficult situation meant I needed to go to the police for resolution. I had to insist on my rights and to do so in a manner that I was wholly unused to. It was excellent training for someone whose boundaries had been routinely and excessively violated.

Appropriate boundaries were just one of the many things that Shiloh spoke of in those few months. He urged me to ask God for anything I wished, saying that if it is God's will then I would receive it.

I believed him. Shiloh's life was proof that all needs were met by God. I could see, quite plainly, that he lived purely by faith.

A few days after he advised me to ask God for whatever I wished, I recall standing on the beach and watching three people kayak out to the reef.

I miss kayaking so much, I thought.

Back when I had a house, a car, and a well-paying job, I owned two kayaks. I yearned for that feeling of sliding silently through the water in the early morning and the sense of freedom it offered.

I reached for my phone to find the nearest water sports rental place—I knew there was one quite close. But Shiloh's words about asking God for everything came to mind. Here was an opportunity to allow God to arrange things for me.

God, I would love to have a kayak trip, if it is Your will. It was such a small thing that I instantly forgot about that minor request, walking on toward home and my editing work that awaited.

The next day, as usual, I sat in the sand for a while in the afternoon staring out at the blue water beyond the reef. A man in a red kayak appeared on the horizon and headed toward the shore. He pulled onto the sand about twenty feet from me, then walked purposefully toward me, asking if I would watch his kayak while he left for a bit.

I agreed. When he returned half an hour later, he carried a large bottle of water that he handed to me thanking me for helping him out.

He began to walk away but then turned back. "Would you like to take it out?"

I accepted his offer, delighted at the quick answer to a tiny prayer. We paddled out over the reef bed where the water deepened to a dark blue and then stopped. Then he handed me a snorkel mask that he scooped from a puddle at his feet. I admitted that it had been twenty years since I last snorkeled but did not mention my life-long fear of deep water.

"Just go," he said, clearly unwilling to consider the idea that swimming near the reef was anything but fantastic. So, I did.

If I had not been underwater, I would have shouted aloud. The most marvelous sight in the world is that of a healthy, thriving reef. For twenty minutes or more I swam, ogling the rainbow of wonders below the water.

Eventually, the man hoisted me back onto the kayak, and we returned to shore.

Not only had God arranged a kayak trip as I had asked, but the answered prayer came with snorkel gear to show me what I had not known to ask for—a glimpse of the incredible reef. Best of all, the beautiful moment unfolded spontaneously. God had placed delights in my path, simply because I had asked.

Later that evening, I met Shiloh for after-dinner tea. I told him about the kayak, barely able to contain my joy at the way it had happened so perfectly and without effort. He rejoiced with me, the lovely way that my request had been answered.

Our conversation sparked a memory. I connected for the first time the prayer I had cast into the sea and Shiloh's arrival one week later.

"Shiloh! I asked God for you!" I exclaimed.

I described the evening to Shiloh, the moment of clarity, next to the sea, explaining that I had been standing there knowing I had no idea what to do with my life when it all felt so pointless. That it seemed the only thing left to do, to ask for a spiritual guide.

I was overcome with the jaw-dropping realization that God had heard me and had sent Shiloh.

He said, "Sophia, God waits endlessly, every moment of every day of every year of every lifetime, for us to ask for help."

God must have indeed been waiting because He swiftly answered my imperfect prayer by sending a faithful messenger. And that messenger had opened my eyes to what I had been blind to for so long. God.

CHAPTER
EIGHT

Despite the ways Egypt had fascinated me, the lovely friends I had made, and the proximity to one of the more gorgeous reefs in the world, I was quite ready to leave.

Shiloh asked me if I knew where I was going to go.

I didn't. I would stay with my son in Texas for a couple of days but he lived in a tiny studio apartment and it would not be comfortable for any longer than that.

I was in the middle of comparing how much money I had in the bank with what I knew it would cost to be back in the United States when Shiloh interrupted my racing thoughts with a question.

As he often did, he cut right to the core of the true issue, which was not anything to do with the superficial aspects of my life—living arrangements or finances or jobs. Instead, he focused me on what I most needed to consider. He asked me what I was afraid of.

His question halted my mental machinations immediately, and I considered it carefully. I was not afraid of being unable to find work if necessary. I could apply for any number of jobs, such was the depth of my work experience. But I had stepped out of full-time work so that I could have a different life, one where I pursued something other than safety. I could not go back to my previous life, not after all that Shiloh had shown me about trusting God and living in faith.

However, I had never had so little money in the bank. I had never had so few prospects for income. With nearly no savings, I lived month to month on sporadic freelance work. It was an uncomfortable existence for someone used to making their own way.

Was I afraid that God didn't care for me as much as he cared for Shiloh? Absolutely. Instead of admitting this, I said what was a little less scary. And no less true.

"Shiloh, I'm afraid I'll be homeless," I said.

"Sophia, can I tell you something? You *are* homeless."

I was stunned to realize that he was absolutely right. I burst out laughing at the irony. The two-month lease on my new apartment was nearly up, and I had nowhere to go, very little money, and no reliable income. Yet, I was perfectly fine.

I never worried about homelessness again. I knew for certain that God would always come through for me. And He always has.

The next week, I sat on a large stone at the edge of the water staring at the mountains of Saudi Arabia in the distance and contemplated my situation. I had two very large, unwieldy suitcases with which I could not easily travel. But more than unburdening myself of things that made travel difficult, I needed to commit to this new life that Shiloh had showed me. After watching him carefully and listening to how much he trusted God to care for his every need, I knew that carrying around so many possessions pointed to a lack of trust.

I began to cry—great wracking sobs. Not out of sadness for the belongings I knew I was going to leave behind, but because I was saying goodbye, forever, to a familiar way of living. I was on the threshold of a new life, and I had no idea what it entailed. All I knew was that I didn't want what was behind me. I wanted what Shiloh had shown me was possible. Peace. Trust. Faith.

CHAPTER
NINE

Much of the next year I spent traveling and house sitting: Scotland, Switzerland, England, and France. The constant moving around kept me from boredom, but also meant a great deal of time alone.

Shiloh had said that understanding myself was a key part of my healing path and being alone accelerated that process. It was far from easy.

The issues that arose were invariably confusing, but when Shiloh guided me through them, I gained new insights into how my experiences skewed my perspectives. The details of how he brought light and healing to my wounds are not possible to repeat. Further, I do not wish to insinuate that anything I experienced is directly applicable for others. Shiloh explained that each of us grows up with a unique history and a unique soul path and only God can guide the healing of each person in the way that is most helpful for them.

Any specific concepts or instructions that Shiloh gave me only serve to illustrate a small portion of the process that was guided by Shiloh and by the circumstances that God sent my way.

Over those years of travel, I tried to implement daily all that Shiloh had taught me: prayer, self-care, self-observation. When I wasn't examining my experiences for clues to incorrect beliefs about myself and the world, I spent much time congratulating myself on living a trusting lifestyle.

My idea of trust in God, however, was rudimentary. I was going to find out soon just how limited in faith I was. The two months that I spent on twenty-two acres of farmland in southern France caring for horses provided the perfect place for me to dig deeply into myself.

After a few weeks, inexplicably, I began to hit my head on the side mirror of the four-wheeler I drove around the paddocks each day while cleaning up after the horses. It was maddening to suddenly be unable to avoid the mirror. The more aware I tried to be, the more I tried to slow down and remind myself it was there, the more aggravating was the next time I smashed my head. Despite my irritation, the symbolism seemed obvious. Anytime you run headlong into a mirror over and over again, there is clearly something you need to see about yourself. Unfortunately, I had no idea what it was.

A week later, things got worse. I began to be stung by wasps, repeatedly and often. The pain was quite long lasting as was the swelling that the stings left behind. Nothing I could do, from diligently seeking out and spraying the multiple nests to wearing layers of protective clothing in the 90-degree heat helped to avoid being stung. Astonishingly, I had never in my life been stung by wasps before, despite ample time spent in nature. I was matter-of-fact about snakes, scorpions, and all manner of insects that inhabit the southern climate I had grown up in. What's more, I encountered many bears in California and swam fearlessly among jellyfish in the Red Sea. However, a month into my summer stay in France, my relationship with nature changed. The instant I opened the door, wasps dove at me. I could even hear them buzzing around my trailer, trying to find a way in.

However, neither the mirror smashing into my head daily nor the constant wasp stings revealed the meaning that both Shiloh and I knew was contained in the situation. Of course,

Shiloh did not tell me the message they brought, though it was one he could see quite plainly. A good teacher does not provide answers.

It was a way of thinking, he said, like a shell around me. He pointed to it, like one would to a bird in the distance. Over and over, patiently, he led me in the direction of the bird, faced me in the right direction, and even handed me binoculars. But he did not describe the bird. He wanted me to learn to find birds myself, even when they hid themselves deeply among the leaves of my consciousness.

One morning I sat at the kitchen table, exhausted from the pain and the monumental frustration of not being able to see the message carried by the wasps and the mirror that seemed destined for my forehead. I desperately wanted to run away as was my habit when faced with truly difficult problems. But this problem I carried within me and no amount of running would resolve it.

Tiredly, I slumped over and propped my chin on my hand. My eyes fell on the bowl of fresh figs that I had gathered early that morning, before the wasps woke up for the day.

I picked up a fig and bit it in half. As I chewed the fresh fruit, I stared at the other half with its red, inner flesh.

Looking closely, I could see that the inside was made of tiny little petals and the tips of some of the petals were a blush of yellow.

I'm not sure what made me pull my laptop close and look up figs. But that's when I discovered that a fig is not a fruit at all. It is a flower. A wasp crawls into a fig, lays eggs, and dies. Baby wasps crawl out and fly away carrying the pollen to another tree.

In a blinding flash of inspiration, I knew why the wasps were stinging me. They wanted me to break open. Only then could my real life, my inner life, blossom and flower. Only then could I grow into who I was meant to be. What I thought was an enemy was my friend, showing me myself.

I also saw what Shiloh had kept pointing to but not naming. It was self-reliance or perhaps pride. I believed that my intelligence and my hard-working nature were keeping me safe. I thought I had money every month because I worked hard for it. I thought I was allowing God to support me, but I was relying on what I had always relied on. Myself.

Shiloh could see that I needed to let go of the spiritual cliff he so often described, the one from which I needed to take a leap of faith and relax in God's perfect care. I had been taking care of myself for so long, with no hope that anyone cared for me, that I didn't recognize the ways that I wasn't allowing God to care for me.

The moment of illumination, the bursting forth of the seed that Shiloh had planted a year earlier was a warm blast filling my body. I tingled with the excitement of understanding. Later, when that amazing moment of discovery no longer covered my skin in prickles of joy, I easily could have begun to doubt its significance. Except for one thing.

I never again bashed my head into the mirror. More incredible, I was never stung again. Once I understood that wasps were attacking me to get me to see that self-reliance limited my trust in God, the wasps never again dive-bombed me as I stepped out of the door. The ominous buzzing that had been growing in fervor around the mobile home completely disappeared.

I hadn't needed to kill wasps. I just needed to receive the message God arranged for them to deliver.

Shiloh, of course, knew all of this and waited patiently for my life experiences to show me what I needed to see. He helped me to see that God cared for me endlessly and magnificently. I stopped trying so hard to find freelance clients and within two months the perfect contract dropped into my lap—a part-time remote position that allowed me freedom of movement and the security of monthly pay.

Two years later, I stood in the bedroom of a house where I was staying in Scotland. I had a bill that I needed to pay and it was substantial. I would need more than my usual monthly work to pay for it, and I had no obvious way to obtain enough money. I looked out the window to the beautiful garden and I said aloud, "God, you know what is needed. Please take care of it. Thank you." I proceeded to knit a wool cap, letting go of the need for money completely.

Within the hour, I received an email from a client I had not heard from for a full year, offering me a large project and a payment that exceeded the waiting bill. It was stunning proof that God does indeed intervene in all aspects of my life just as Shiloh had always assured me.

CHAPTER
TEN

It took me years to realize how profoundly Shiloh understood my wounding. Eventually, however, it dawned on me the mastery he had displayed not just in understanding me but in knowing how to address the particular nuances of what made me so distrustful. He had known all along how ready I was to run, even when I didn't know it myself.

I thanked him for being so careful with me, acknowledging the skill it required. I was not surprised at all when he said that God shows him everything he needs to know, declining to take even an ounce of credit. His adeptness in healing my psychological wounds was surpassed only by his humility before God.

One day, when I was ready to listen without self-judgment,

he explained a divine perspective of difficult circumstances, one that showed me a purpose for all that I had been through. The view he offered did not involve blame but the understanding that everything was arranged for my soul's benefit. As he spoke, answering my many questions before I could even ask them, I could feel myself releasing the deep anger of a victim.

As he spoke, his total lack of judgment, particularly of everyone I had blamed for hurting me, snapped something deep inside. Finally I could move beyond the difficult childhood that made me distrust everyone.

That marked a new threshold of trust for me and set the stage for all that would come next.

After a year or so of travel, I returned to the States where I spent the next six months. I bought a used car and eventually drove to Santa Fe, one of my favorite places and where I had lived for three years. I arranged to rent a room from a friend who owned a lovely house in the desert, and the following day, stopped by my former workplace to see whether they needed a substitute teacher.

Instead, they offered me a full-time teaching position.

My intent had been to work one day a week, at most,

while trying to figure out where to go next. But here was an interesting opportunity. Fond memories as a teacher at that school tugged at my heart. I longed for a place where I could feel settled.

The school year was just about to begin, and they gave me a few days to accept or decline the position. I headed to my room in the house in the desert and promptly flew into a panic. I huddled on the floor of the bathroom, shaking. Something was not right. After a few minutes of the mystifying reaction, I contacted Shiloh, who luckily was available despite the time difference.

"Shiloh, something is very wrong. Very wrong."

I wasn't sure why, but often when I spoke with Shiloh I became quite clear on how I felt about things. Today was no different. Shiloh asked me a series of questions and each time I answered, it brought me closer to realizing that a full-time teaching position didn't feel right at all. I had thought that I should take the job because it seemed so serendipitous, so synchronistic, and such an easy thing to do because I was here. But when I finally admitted to myself that taking the job felt like a mistake, Shiloh explained that sometimes things occur just to remind us what we do not want. I felt profound relief. I had been close to doing something that I didn't want to do because someone had asked me to. Pleasing others was an old pattern for me.

I hung up, glad that I was clear on rejecting the job. But the feeling of near panic continued.

I felt an urgency to leave—to get out. Immediately. I had no idea where it was coming from but it was nearly uncontrollable and I began to pack my things. It didn't take long. I told the friend from whom I had rented the room that I was leaving. I tried to come up with an explanation but truthfully, I had no real idea why I was leaving. I just had to go, and soon.

Within half an hour of beginning to pack, I found out why. My youngest sister, who lived south of Houston, texted me.

"Sophia, I am in the hospital. There's no one to take care of the kids and Chris has to go out of town for work."

"I'm on my way," I texted back. "I was already packing."

CHAPTER
ELEVEN

After staying with my sister and her family for six weeks, it was time to leave though I had nowhere to go nor any idea of a direction. I packed up my car and drove to the coast where I slept in the car on the beach. The weather in Texas is often mild, even in winter, so it was fairly comfortable. I spent days in a cafe working and afternoons walking along the shore. After several days, Shiloh texted me to see how I was doing.

"I've told God that I'm not moving from this beach until He tells me where to go." I was determined to wait for divine direction.

I thought my intention admirable until Shiloh pointed out gently that giving God an ultimatum was perhaps not the best way to go about receiving guidance. Instead, he suggested that I accept whatever occurred and be open to hearing God's directions, which may come in subtle ways and at a time that was not mine to know or predict.

I would have laughed at myself except it was such a monumental misunderstanding. Instead of demanding an answer, I needed to have patience. I needed to trust all that God arranged for my life in the timing in which He arranged it.

I awoke the next day, hopeful for some feeling, a nudge in any direction. As I stepped out of the car onto the sand, I found a small group of blackbirds, quite close to the car, regarding me calmly. They didn't fly off when I slammed the door. As I sat in my folding chair on the sand facing the water, they stared at me, unmoving,

I had breakfast, cleaned up the car, and went to the cafe to work as was my habit, leaving the staring blackbirds behind. As soon as I parked in the lot of the cafe, a blackbird landed on the hood of my car and looked at me through the windshield. Once inside, the barista recognized me.

"The WiFi isn't working, just so you know. We can't figure out why." I thanked her and ordered my tea to go. With my usual routine of working at the cafe blocked, I returned to the car where the blackbird was still sitting on my hood. As I approached, he began to flap his wings and caw, loudly and persistently, remaining on the hood all the while.

His odd behavior along with the discomfort of trying to

live in my car was the nudge I needed. I drove back to my sister's house. A few days later, I woke up one morning with the idea to go to Spain. It seemed as good a destination as any, mostly because I speak the language. I made a plane reservation. Within a week, I was gone.

A nomadic life sounds quite romantic but long-term it presents difficulties. I could never own anything more than what I could carry. I could never get truly comfortable in a place or establish new friendships. I became tired of throwing things away—jackets, shoes, toiletries—that I could not fit into my suitcase when it was time to move on.

When I went to Spain, I secretly hoped I could apply for a long-term visa. Maybe I could stay for a year. Or more.

Once in Spain, though, nothing worked out. Even finding the kind of food I wanted was inexplicably difficult. My hotel room did not have a desk, and I was not comfortable spending the entire day working at a cafe. I tried to be patient and trust that something would arise.

Three weeks before Christmas, Shiloh called. We chatted for a few minutes, and eventually, I told him of the difficult time I was having in settling in. What he said next surprised me so much that I thought I heard wrong.

"Would you like to live on my boat?"

I began to laugh, then stopped abruptly. "Wait—you're serious?"

"Why not?" He had bought a boat and renovated it.

All of a sudden, it seemed a magnificent idea. I told him that I was meeting my son in England for Christmas and New Year. I could go to the south coast of England to see the boat after that.

Remarkably, a few weeks later, I was living on Shiloh's boat in the marina. Her name was Sirius and she was quite comfortable. It was incredible, the work he had done. He bought her to bring her back to life and reversed the years in which she had been allowed to sit uncared for. She was not huge but large enough for comfort. She had a berth in the bow and a galley with a seating area. The wheelhouse was large enough for yoga and had several seating places.

Sirius was a perfect place for me to rest for a while. Within a few weeks, I found out how perfect. The pandemic closed borders all over the world. I, who traveled as a lifestyle, would have been in a great deal of trouble without a place to stay.

Shiloh painstakingly showed me how to take care of Sirius. I was not good at it. The manual sea toilet mystified me. I was afraid to peek into the bilges, which seemed dank and dirty. I was reluctant to start the engine, a task so daunting that I avoided it as long as possible.

Slowly, through great effort and much coaching, I became used to the boat, her sounds, and her particular needs. One morning, I opened my eyes, and the ceiling over my head seemed incredibly far away. How bizarre to have a sense of space in such a physically close environment. Shiloh said that Sirius was magical that way.

"She has such a beautiful energy," he would say.

All I knew was that I felt safe on Sirius. I thought it was because she was Shiloh's. How could he own something that did not have a beautiful energy?

As the spring neared its end and the pandemic continued, I began to be nervous about my visa, which was soon to expire. I had nowhere to go. The US was expensive, and I had no home there.

I was granted a visa extension based on the pandemic. Eventually, however, even that extension played out and I was forced to look for a place to go. I settled on a southern European country. I imagined I would find a small town where I could stay for a few months quite inexpensively and enjoy the countryside. I found an apartment online and booked a place for six weeks.

Shiloh drove to the marina to say goodbye and make sure the boat was secure enough to be left unattended. As we ate dinner that night, he said that if I needed to come back, then Sirius would be there for me.

I didn't see that happening. "Thank you, Shiloh, but I'm ready to move on. Kind of done with the UK, you know?" In any case, my visa was up and it would be six months before I would be allowed back in.

Then he repeated that I could return to Sirius if I needed to. I should have paid closer attention.

CHAPTER
TWELVE

Once my plane landed, I handed my passport to the border patrol agent, who took one look at the golden eagle stamped on the front and stood up.

"Come with me."

Four hours later, after waiting in a room with twenty or thirty other unlucky souls, I had an official interview. The interviewing officer frowned at me.

"Your last stamp was entry into Spain. Then, nothing. Where have you been?"

"I went to the UK," I said. "They don't stamp US passports there." It was true. Americans enter the UK through an automated process.

He grew stern. "Then you have overstayed in the UK.

You are only allowed three months and it has been much longer. We cannot allow you to enter when you have over-stayed in another EU country."

I struggled to quell my irritation. "That's not true. Americans can stay in the UK for six months." I didn't even try to tell him about the extension I had received.

He flapped his hand dismissively at me. "We still think of the UK as part of the EU." Membership in the EU has nothing to do with the Schengen agreement, which governs entry into a subset of nations. He was confusing these two things and a border agent should know better.

"The UK is not part of the Schengen—," I began, but he held up his hand looking down at a paper on his desk.

He was not listening. I leaned back in my chair, defeated but unrepentant, and I stopped trying to be reasonable and polite.

"Look, I accept that you are not allowing me into the country," I snapped. "But I am not going to allow you to accuse me of overstaying in a country where I did not over-stay. I am no more a COVID risk than anyone else in the UK. So, unless you block all Americans no matter where they are coming from, you'll have to come up with some other reason for denying me entry."

He did. He checked two boxes on my official interview form, one that said I was a risk for working in the country and one that said I could not prove that I was going to leave. Both were technically true—as true as they are with any country that I have ever visited.

I was ushered out of the office and into a hallway, where I stood awaiting direction as to my next move. Somehow, I accidentally stepped beyond an invisible line.

"Stop! You can't go there!" Confused, I turned around, not sure what I had done wrong.

Angrily, the guard rushed over, "I didn't say you could leave!" Once again, I felt the sting of being accused of something that I had not done. With little attempt at civility, he escorted me down an array of hallways to the detention area.

The seating area was equipped with cast-off banks of airport seats and a vending machine that accepted cash payment only. The sleeping room labeled "Men" was lined with well-used cots. The dingy, white walls had a gray, oily sheen where hundreds of people had leaned against the wall. Cameras focused on every area of the dim room.

The restroom door had a hole in it where the handle should have been. It stood ajar at least two inches, the interior visible in the seating area where other detainees awaited their fate. But worse than the lack of privacy was the lack of soap. Despite complaining, nothing changed.

I shared my phone charger with another traveler who spoke no English. He left after a few hours, nodding to me on his way out, suitcase in tow. It reminded me that I had no idea where my bag was.

I approached the guard station to inquire about my suitcase and when I might be allowed to leave. I noticed a man standing behind the window of a tiny chamber directly across from the guard post. I recognized him; we had chatted briefly before our detention while waiting for our official interviews.

He was separated from the rest of us, in a dark and tiny chamber with nothing but a cot. He had only a view of the guard who paid him no attention. His eyes held panic and unshed tears. My heart clenched in sympathy.

"Why are you in there?" I asked.

His lips moved in response, but I could not hear him. I retrieved my writing notebook from my backpack. I turned to a clean page, wrote my question, and held it up for him to see.

I wanted to say something to him, to provide some human contact, some compassion, when everything else had been ripped away.

From behind me, the bald guard sitting at his desk began yelling, "What are you doing? Get away from there. You cannot talk to him!"

I blinked, turning toward him as he approached me. "Why not?"

I still did not fully understand my prisoner status.

"I don't have to tell you anything," he sneered, as he ripped the notebook from my hands.

He forestalled my protestations with more shouting. "No! You don't speak! You sit down! Over there, in that chair."

The hours of waiting without water or food, the tenuousness of my situation, the lack of sleep from the night before when I was preparing for the trip, and now this nonsense—it was too much to bear. I lost my temper. "*That* chair? Do I have to sit in *that* chair? What about this chair? Or this one?"

"If you don't sit down in that chair," he yelled, pointing to a specific chair across the room, "I'm going to treat you like the American police treat Americans." George Floyd had just been murdered by police in Minnesota, sparking worldwide protests.

I quivered with indignation. I had done absolutely nothing to deserve such treatment. Could he not see that man was suffering from a form of torture, for doing nothing but getting on an airplane? Was this guard truly threatening me with harm for no reason other than speaking to a fellow traveler?

With effort, I clamped my mouth shut, walked across the room, and sat down, avoiding the chair he had indicated. My tiny mutiny against his unreasonable demand did not go unnoticed.

He called out, "I could make you wait a long time for your flight out."

He did. Other detainees came and went within hours. Not me. Later, when he was no longer focused on me, I went to the sleeping area and tilted one of the cots to shake out the crumbs.

I sat on the cot with my scarf over my head to escape the constant gaze of the guards and the security cameras. I craved privacy intensely. To be able to have an unnoticed expression on my face. To yawn privately. To gaze at something unobserved. It is difficult to explain the humiliation of being on constant display.

The lights, the snoring of the other detainees, the discomfort of sleeping on a dirty cot without a pillow or cover, and the guards laughing at the vending machine not six feet from my head kept me awake.

Another day and another night passed. I didn't know when I would be allowed to leave. I became used to the room, the cot, the bank of chairs, the lack of soap, my bad breath. They asked me what I wanted to eat. I told them I was vegetarian, and they brought fish sandwiches which I declined. I quelled my hunger with water. I lost all sense of time and urgency.

Early on the morning of the third day, a guard approached my cot. I was not asleep.

"You are leaving in two hours."

I visited the bathroom with the hole in the door. I arranged my hair the best I could with no mirror and no brush. Then I sat on the edge of the cot and waited.

A new guard came, one who smiled. He escorted me out of the detention area. "Where is your luggage?" he asked.

"I don't know," I said. "I figured the airline has it." I did not tell him that I had been threatened with violence when I tried to ask about it. He looked surprised, then doubtful. His doubt was well founded. Despite myriad and lengthy attempts with the airline to locate the suitcase over the next weeks, I never saw it again, nor was I ever compensated for the loss of everything I owned.

We walked, him in front and another armed guard behind, as though I might try to escape. To further my humiliation, I was led under armed guard onto the nearly empty plane and made to sit well apart from all the other passengers in the half-full plane.

The agent who had escorted me to my seat handed the flight attendant a plastic bag containing my passport. My insides clenched spasmodically despite my empty stomach. I had not known the meaning I had placed in that little booklet. Without realizing it, I had abdicated my identity as though it were something that existed outside of me.

I folded up the armrest and lay down across two seats. They were vastly cleaner than anything I had seen in the detention room. I slept.

When we landed in the UK, I waited while those with passports deplaned. Finally, a border patrol agent stepped onto the plane and motioned me to come forward. The flight attendant handed my passport to him and his waiting companion. We walked through the airport, side by side. No one yelled at me.

"What happened?" he said kindly, as though I were a friend.

I tried to explain the whole thing, that they had accused me first of not being in the UK for any length of time and then, conversely, of overstaying. He was sympathetic.

"That must have been upsetting."

His friendly manner and benign questions lulled me into a feeling of safety and I rewarded him with a precise summary of all that had happened. I didn't realize until I was halfway through it, that our conversation was an interview. I didn't care. I had nothing to hide.

He determined the size of my bank account and my profession and asked about my grown children. I couldn't help mentioning the irrelevant affront that was the absence of soap several times, and then, the fateful detail about the lack of a UK entry stamp in my passport.

He agreed that the UK practice of not stamping US passports could be problematic.

"Even when people ask for it, we are not allowed to give

it," he said regretfully. "But we cannot let you into the UK because your visa here has expired."

"But I have nowhere to go," I protested weakly. "And my suitcase is gone. I don't even have a change of clothes." I was hungry and exhausted and I badly needed a shower.

He nodded sympathetically. After speaking with his boss, he turned back to me. "You will need to buy a ticket to somewhere outside the EU. Then, we can let you in the UK for a short time to get yourself situated."

I sat on the tiled floor near an outlet, charging my computer enough to buy a ticket to the closest place I could find that would allow me to enter and where I could afford to live.

Then it was done. I showed him my plane ticket for a flight seven days from then. I packed my laptop into my backpack, and he walked with me to the exit. As I passed through the gate, another agent handed me my passport with a smile.

I was free.

When I texted Shiloh, he responded right away that I could stay on Sirius. I recalled his parting words had been to assure me that I could return to the boat if needed. Naively, I had thought him kind, rather than prophetic.

Once settled on the train, I opened my passport. I saw a large X through the port of entry stamp.

I don't know what made me turn the page.

There, in the center of the next page, was a large stamp indicating a UK port of entry and the words "Leave to enter for 6 months" with the current date. I read it three times before understanding that I could stay in the UK. Someone had bent the rules. I'm not sure if it was because of my bank account, my profession, or sheer pity at my sorry state, but I didn't have to leave.

I swore to myself that I would never again ignore anything that Shiloh told me.

CHAPTER
THIRTEEN

Those first few days back on the boat glowed golden. It was freedom, I think. Freedom to walk where I wished, to eat when hungry, to move about unobserved, to speak to whom I wished.

I reveled in each moment, though I had lost all of my clothes, shoes, jewelry, mementos of my prior life. Save my computer, everything I owned was in that missing suitcase. Yet, each breath felt like a sparkling treasure. I could not recall ever feeling so perfectly content. To my delight, I discovered that all I truly needed was clean air, clean food, clean clothes, and a place to sleep. Everything else was nice but unnecessary.

Shiloh had said that difficult circumstances were gifts, but

I hadn't known what he meant. If he had told me that losing everything I owned and being humiliated and threatened by an armed guard would be the catalyst for such a joyful perspective, I would never have believed it.

After changing into some newly purchased clothes, I stood in the marina laundry room to wash the clothes I had worn for several days. After inserting my coins into the machine, the digital counter showed that I lacked ten pence. I was so certain that I had enough money that I stared for quite a while in disbelief. Then I began to search the floor. I knew there had to be ten pence somewhere. God always provided what I needed, Shiloh had asserted many times. It had become a mantra for me. If it were true, then there was ten pence in my immediate proximity.

I opened the door and looked outside on the jetty. Nothing. I closed the door of the laundry room and I stood there again with my eyes closed. I could feel the ten pence. I knew with total certainty that all I needed was here, in front of me, in this moment. I dropped to my hands and knees and peered underneath the washing machine. It was hideously dirty with dust and fuzz and grime. Nothing else.

I stood again, eyes closed, and total calmness flowed into my heart. The certainty that God provided all I needed filled me.

I walked to the other side of the washers, where only a

small portion of the side of one washer was visible. I again dropped to my knees and peered underneath. There was not a speck of dirt, and just under the edge of the washer, I was delighted to see a shiny coin. I picked it up. Ten pence.

About three days later, during a thoroughly enjoyable shower at the marina facilities, my joyous state continued. The warm water, the soap, the privacy, the cleanliness still delighted me. Those things had never meant much before, but now I rejoiced in the delicious feeling of the warm water pouring over my shoulders. That is when I heard, quite clearly, a message. A directive from God.

"Buy Sirius."

It was as though a door had opened and a shaft of light wrapped in utter bliss had fallen on me. Then just as quickly, it closed. Not only had I heard the message that was delivered in that quick moment, I had felt the accompanying rush of elation that I knew was the unmistakable hallmark of the Divine.

I gasped. How perfect! I'll buy Sirius!

As I dried off and dressed, I began to think about what buying Sirius might mean. Buying her would be expensive. I had no means to keep a boat. I could not drive her. I didn't live in the UK. I knew nothing about boats or boat engines.

For the first time in many years, I was debt-free. I had money in the bank. Not a fortune, but more than I had been able to save in a long time. Enough to feel secure. Enough that I did not concern myself with my next paycheck.

Shiloh had been urging me for years to surrender to God. Up to now, surrender meant waiting for guidance and accepting circumstances that came my way. This was different. Now I was to surrender to God for something I did not want and that made absolutely no sense. Though I did not understand the reason for this directive, I knew I would comply. If I wished to be on a path of surrender to God, how could I possibly say no?

Shiloh sat across from me a few evenings later in the boat. I knew how much he had labored to bring her back to life. She had been in a terrible state and now she was whole and beautiful.

"Shiloh, I am ready to buy Sirius if you feel it is right to sell her to me."

"There is something important in this. I can't quite see what it is, but I trust that it will become clear in time," he said. He agreed to sell her to me if I gave him the right of first refusal if ever I decided to sell her.

I readily agreed. With that, we signed the papers.

I arranged to have Sirius lifted from the water and placed in the boatyard so I could clean and repaint the hull and wheelhouse and apply anti-foul below the waterline. Sirius spent three weeks on dry land while I scraped and painted and made other minor repairs.

I went from owning only a laptop and a backpack to owning a boat. It was quite a shift. When I purchased Sirius, I emptied my savings account. It was not as much as she was worth, but it was all I had. I was back to living paycheck to paycheck.

Two and half months into the surreal life of owning a boat that I didn't know how to sail, I awoke at 1:30 AM. I do not typically have trouble sleeping and I lay there in the quiet, wondering what had awakened me so thoroughly.

As though in answer, I heard clearly another divine message.

"Give Sirius back."

The words sounded like the ringing of a beautiful bell and were accompanied by a feeling of intense joy and happiness. Although it was the same process that had occurred when I had been instructed to buy Sirius, the directive was even more clear and there was even more joy. This time I skipped the mental evaluation of the repercussions. My surrender was immediate.

I began to laugh. I had just bought a boat and sunk a fair

bit of money into repairs and upkeep, and now I was giving it up.

Immediately, a feeling of deep gravity settled over me, and in it a reproof—a correction. There was absolutely nothing funny about the process of learning to surrender to God's will. I should honor the sacred lesson it was.

I lay there for a few minutes asking to understand all that was happening. I waited, still feeling the joy washing over me.

In the darkness and the quiet space of acceptance, understanding bloomed. I had lost everything when I was detained at the airport. Except my bank account. With my savings, I effortlessly replaced my clothes and other minor belongings. What need had I to trust God when I had money? If I stored up physical possessions to protect myself against difficult circumstances, where was God in my life? If I continued to find my security in human things there was no room for God.

I was asked to give up Sirius and the money I had invested in her so that I could fully experience surrender and trust in divine providence. I understood it was the only way that God could show me how perfectly He cared for me.

A sense of euphoria descended when I realized that here was my opportunity to place myself in God's hands. I felt nothing but the greatest happiness. Absolute total bliss.

As soon as it was a decent hour, I called Shiloh.

"God woke me last night, in the middle of the night. He told me to give Sirius back to you."

"Are you sure?"

"Shiloh, I can't have misinterpreted the message."

Further, the feeling I had when I considered it was absolute and total joy.

I cannot adequately describe the incredible feeling that came over me when I surrendered to God in this. It was unlike anything I had ever experienced in my life. Shiloh, sensitive as he was, could feel the bliss that surrendering to God's request brought to me.

This experience had nothing to do with owning a boat or finances or logic. This was a moment in which I had been asked to trust God fully. To trust God's voice and God's direction and God's plan entirely without question.

Shiloh said, "Sophia, I am being shown that some part of you when you were very young, wondered what God was. Wanted to know the truth of God. Now, here is the answer for you. You have been given the gift of faith."

After we spoke, the whole day continued to feel indescribably magical. Every moment was beautiful. Each time I thought of giving Sirius back to Shiloh, a perfect peace rose inside me.

A few days later, there was more. I was typing, doing some work, and the message came to me.

"Pay for Sirius' berthing."

I froze with my hands above the keyboard, knowing how perfectly correct it was. Then, I understood fully. I was to live on Sirius, care for Sirius, and pay the monthly fees. But she was not mine.

That is how things worked out. I lived on Sirius when I was in the UK. I understood that this had been God's plan all along. But I needed to be brought along slowly. Each step along the way was a test. Would I listen to God? Would I allow God to be in control? Or would I revert to thinking I was in control? Would I turn to human things for security or would I turn to He Who provides everything I truly need?

Much later, when all was settled, I asked Shiloh what it had been like for him.

"I was just observing the process. I trusted that God had a plan."

Then he said that Sirius was a very special boat, filled with light. A safe haven whose importance would become clear, in time.

When I first moved aboard Sirius, many months passed before I could force myself to pull up the floorboards in the wheelhouse and look into the bilge space underneath. The dark damp area seemed so dirty and repulsive.

Eventually, a musty, moldy odor began greeting me when I opened the door. I finally was able to locate the source in a cabinet in the boat's galley area. I tried to clean it but the smell persisted. Finally, I pulled away the board that formed the back of the cabinet to reveal a huge colony of black mold.

I spent several hours scrubbing and scraping with various cleaning supplies. I cried the entire time. I do not typically cry while I am cleaning, so I knew something in myself needed clearing as well. It wasn't too difficult to understand the message once I looked for it: hidden things fester badly, both in the boat and inside me.

After I finished removing the mold, I painted the inside of the cabinet a light blue. The smell was gone and it would never return.

The message was not lost on me. I should open up all the places inside myself that I was too afraid to look at. Interestingly, my perception of the bilges changed entirely. They were not dark and scary—just unloved.

CHAPTER
FOURTEEN

Not long after returning to Sirius after the border detention, I experienced a protracted bout of food poisoning. Three weeks of forced fasting passed before I recovered enough to eat. Once I felt strong enough, I headed out for a much-needed walk, a nature gift to myself for recovery and, coincidentally, for my birthday. I chose a route that led into the countryside, rambling in a large circle over hilly ground. I had walked nearly two miles when I came upon a large snail making its slow way across the path. I stopped, inexplicably riveted by this determined little creature. The snail ignored me, even when I stroked its shell. I should have minded its message more carefully.

Not five minutes later, on a muddy downslope, my left

foot slipped. I fell forward over my rigidly stuck right foot, and my shin approached the top of my boot in a distinctly abnormal way, crunching the arch.

Despite the pain, I hauled myself up and took a few steps but I knew instantly the injury was worse than any I'd ever had. Providentially, the week before, Shiloh had told me the emergency number for the UK. I sat at the edge of the path and dialed 999. I wasn't entirely sure where I was but I described the location of the trailhead and what I could see. The dispatcher said they would send an ambulance. An hour later, with no help in sight, I began to shake with cold.

There seemed no choice but to get myself to the road. In the continuing drizzle, I began a three-pointed crab walk, with one foot in the air. After about an hour of the crab walk, my arms grew so tired that I could no longer hold myself up. I sat on the edge of the path, soaked, and decided enough was enough. Surely I could manage the minor pain of a twisted ankle and walk the remaining half mile to the road.

I was part hopping and part hobbling when I came to the road. Emergency services had just arrived and the driver helped me the final few steps into the waiting ambulance.

Once in the packed emergency room, I sat in a wheelchair for four and a half hours. Eventually, I was wheeled back to the doctor, who after thirty seconds of looking at my sausage-shaped foot, ordered a radiograph. Soon enough, I was again taken back to speak with him. He held up the black and white film and pointed to a long thin bone, clearly broken in two.

"That is a broken metatarsal."

I jumped a bit at his words. Two weeks earlier Shiloh had called and unexpectedly had asked whether I had ever broken my foot. When I told him, that I had never broken anything at all he said, "I keep hearing 'broken metatarsal, broken metatarsal' and I thought it may be in relation to you." Shiloh had given me the warning that he had received in the most positive way possible, but foolishly, I had thought nothing of it. Again, I felt chagrin at underestimating his prescience.

But the doctor wasn't finished. "You also have hairline fractures in two other bones." He pointed to tiny lines in the two block-type bones that form the arch. "We won't know yet whether you need surgery. Sometimes this kind of break heals badly and surgery is needed."

Back in the waiting area, I asked for help in calling a taxi, and the intake person, overwhelmed with a full ER on a Sunday evening, pointed to the phone on the wall. It said, "This phone rings a taxi service only." I stood there balancing painfully for nearly a half hour with the phone to my ear. No one answered.

I carefully crutched outside and sat in a plastic chair by

the door in the light rain. It was 10:30 PM. I was alone, in pain, hungry, tired, and dangerously dehydrated. Several attempts to call a taxi with my cell phone had been unsuccessful. Further, my ride service app was not working because my account had been irretrievably hacked the previous year when I was in France.

Finally, I texted Shiloh, the only person in the country whose phone number I had.

"Hello, Shiloh, are you anywhere near Brighton?"

But he was not.

I described my ordeal and the unsuccessful taxi-calling attempts to Shiloh and then put my phone into my damp pocket. I sat in the rain and, lacking any other recourse or even strength to think, I asked God for help.

Within a few minutes, two men approached the door, and seeing me looking quite miserable, they stopped.

"Are you okay?"

I shook my head, unable to speak. I was dangerously close to wailing.

"Do you need some help?" the younger man persisted.

"I can't seem to get a taxi." A tear of utter exhaustion rolled down my face. I'm not sure if they noticed in the dark and the rain.

"My wife is in labor," he said. "But I can help you get a taxi." He spent the next twenty minutes on the phone calling several different taxi services. At one point he looked up, and said, apologetically, "There is a festival, so all the taxis are busy."

I nodded. I no longer cared. My taxi was no longer my concern. I had given it to God to handle.

Finally, he announced that my ride would arrive in thirty minutes, and I thanked him for his persistence.

It was nearly midnight when I finally crawled aboard the boat that I had left so cheerfully that morning. I lay for hours in the berth, exhausted, but unable to sleep. I had no pain medication and no way to get any. The bones in my foot were like red hot pokers.

Pain can be a great lesson, Shiloh had once told me. I had not known what he meant. Pain seemed a thing to address, much like an empty stomach or dirty laundry. But with no recourse, I had to accept the pain as part of a natural healing process. Pain would not, in itself, hurt me. Mental fortitude, it seemed, was the lesson that pain brought.

Eventually, in the early hours of the morning, I slept.

Late morning of the next day, Shiloh arrived. He had driven several hours out of his way to drop off food and stayed long enough to be sure I had what I needed. Without his kindness, I'm not sure how I would have managed that first week while I was working out how to survive these new painfully awkward circumstances.

Shiloh stopped by for another short visit about six weeks later. I had discovered that I did not require surgery and the bruises on my abdomen from the injections of blood thinner were slowly disappearing.

Nodding to my still swollen foot in its boot, he said, "I think you will look back at this and find that this was a turning point for you."

"I keep wondering why this happened. Shiloh, I never fall. It is just not something I do. I have hiked much more dangerous paths in truly difficult conditions. This was barely a hike. More like a walk down a country path."

"What do you think?" he asked.

I tried to think of what could have happened. Finally, I shook my head. "I don't know. I was planning to go to Portugal the next week. I was so happy about the apartment on the beach I had found."

"Sophia, where did God wish you to be?"

It was the perfect question. Without realizing it, I had gone off God's path and onto my own. I tried to trace how I had gotten to that point, to see where I had started to think I was following God's guidance when I was not.

"I thought I was to go to Portugal. It is much cheaper

than here and things lined up so nicely. I felt so happy about it."

Shiloh understood. He knew that my wishes could easily override the sometimes subtle whispers of God working in my life. With patience, he deftly described again how to practice discernment and to differentiate between my mind's wishes and God's will.

When he told me that patience was key, I couldn't believe how I had missed my own impatience. The inexplicably fascinating snail on the trail that day now seemed less an accidental encounter than pointed instruction.

Knowing my intensely self-critical tendency, Shiloh assured me that all was well. "You have done nothing wrong. This was just a correction. When God needs you to be in one place and you try to go to another, then He stops you."

I understood. I had interfered in a divine plan that I knew nothing about.

"You must be careful, Sophia. Corrections will get more pronounced."

CHAPTER
FIFTEEN

The week after Thanksgiving, I was awakened in the middle of the night by a movie playing in my head. I recognized it.

Many years earlier the first two chapters of a science fiction book for kids popped into my mind, like a gift, fully packaged. But beyond those first chapters, nothing happened. Every few years I would revisit it, to see whether anything would come of it. Nothing ever did.

On this night, however, the next scene in the book appeared in my head, rolling like a video. I got up, opened my laptop, and wrote for two hours. Then the strange movie stopped. It was 4:00 AM, and I went back to bed.

Two hours later I got up and worked a full day. When I

went to bed that night, I had no idea I would not sleep for long. About two hours into an exhausted sleep the movie again began to play. Again, I leaped from bed to record it. This time it lasted three hours. I typed nonstop without looking up and when it stopped, I fell asleep for a short time before, once again, working a full day. The middle-of-the-night writing repeated for two weeks. I was working all day and then writing at night. I developed a terrible cold.

"Please. Please, I need to sleep. Why not wake me up at 6:00 AM after I have slept?" I begged whoever was in charge for respite.

That night, I collapsed into bed and fell asleep instantly. After a full night's sleep, I was awakened at 6:00 AM with the next chapter. Elated, I wrote for two hours until once again the movie switched off, and I began to work.

After a few weeks, the movie began playing at random moments during the day. Once, when I was walking from the jetty after a shower, the last chapter appeared, though it was out of sequence. I ran to capture it, fearful that it would disappear before I could write it down.

"Shiloh, this is the most fascinating process!" I said, when next we spoke. I described how I could somewhat control when the movie played but that I had started to receive the second book at the same time as the first and it was getting confusing.

Shiloh told me, then, that he could see there would be three books. They would be initially intertwined but I would separate them as I moved forward. It was gratifying to hear what he saw as the outcome of this fascinating writing endeavor.

"Sophia, I'm not sure that this could have happened anywhere else except on Sirius," he said.

Not only did I feel Sirius to be supportive, I believed Shiloh. I knew he could see and feel things that I could not. I felt incredibly fortunate and grateful to God for arranging it all, and particularly for preventing me from leaving for Portugal.

The all-consuming process continued. In mid-December, as the intense writing continued, the sea toilet on the boat stopped working. I reluctantly earmarked an entire Saturday to fix it.

When Saturday arrived, I spent much of the day running back and forth from the boat to the chandlery in the marina for toilet replacement parts, pipes, and other supplies. I replaced the entire toilet pump mechanism. It still did not work. Then I pulled up all the boards covering the bilge where the extractor pipe was. I knew it had to be clogged. Removing it was complicated because of the various places it traversed—none were easily accessible.

I pushed and pulled and tugged and sweated. For two

hours I struggled to remove that pipe. It would not budge. When I finally cut one end of the pipe off the seacock, it was almost completely filled with the hard substance that forms when urine comes into contact with salt water. No wonder the pipe resisted being removed—it was like trying to bend concrete.

Eventually, I realized there was no way for me to remove that pipe by myself. I needed someone to guide and pull as I pushed it around several bends. I didn't know anyone well enough to ask for help with a sewage pipe. I sat for a few minutes, breathing hard from the exertion.

There was only one thing I could do.

God, I need help. I don't know what to do.

After this brief request for help, I stood up, washed my hands, and pushed aside the tools on the table to clear a small space where I placed a napkin. I had not eaten yet that day. I turned on some music, averted my eyes from the chaos, and began to eat.

Before I finished the meal, a loud knock sounded on the boat.

No one had knocked on the boat in the two years I had been on and off Sirius. I went to the wheelhouse and peeked out.

A man stood on the pontoon. I recognized him from the chandlery.

"Yes?" I asked.

"I was just checking to see how it was going for you."

My mouth dropped open. *God works fast*, I thought.

I invited him into the mess. "It's not going well. I could use another set of hands."

He came in and set to removing that pipe with gusto. I was right, though. There was no way I could have done it myself and he couldn't either. Together, after about an hour of cutting, tugging, pushing, and pulling that pipe was removed.

The next day after I finished connecting the final pipe to the toilet, I called Shiloh.

"It is done. And it works perfectly." I was elated and told him of the help I had received when I most needed it.

"Well done," he said. "God always comes through for us. Always. The most important thing is to ask for help. How is the writing going?"

"It is amazing. I think it won't be too long before I am finished."

After we hung up, an incredible realization dawned.

Although I had made the right decision in abandoning teaching as a career, I missed very much helping children navigate the process of growing up. God knew the yearnings of my heart, particularly my wish to help children deal with challenging feelings. For the first time, I saw that these novels for children were a new way for me to help kids, one that was outside the confines of curricular materials. Suddenly, it was more than a book series. It was the answer to a heart's wish.

CHAPTER
SIXTEEN

S ome months later Shiloh was in town and asked if I wished to join him for dinner. That evening, as we waited for our food, I recall looking up at him and feeling something quite strange.

"Shiloh, it feels like you are seeing right to the back of my head and down inside me."

He looked away, possibly to spare me the intensity of his direct gaze. I was not the first to tell him this. It is true, he said, explaining that when he looks at someone, he not only sees who that person is at a deep level, but he sees the reasons why they are who they are.

This feeling of being deeply known had been my experience of Shiloh for several years. However, we had not seen each other for many months. I had forgotten what it was like to be truly seen.

I asked how he was able to do this, to see into the essence of others. His answer, I cannot repeat here in full. But he said the key to seeing the truth of any situation or any person was to lack judgment.

"How is it possible to be so completely nonjudgmental?" I didn't feel that I judged others. I was sure I must be doing it all the time without intending to.

First, he said, we must forgive ourselves for anything we think we have done wrong.

Into my mind immediately sprang the one thing I had not been able to forgive myself for. Ben's suicide.

Shiloh had spoken with me about Ben many times. I still clung to the idea that I didn't deserve happiness or forgiveness when Ben had been so miserable. I believed that there was something I could have done, but didn't, that would have saved him.

Shiloh did not try to argue my innocence or show me that I lacked the power to affect the course of others' lives. He did not try to convince me that the situation was complex or that I was blameless. Instead, he said something quite life-changing—that there was nothing to forgive myself for. He explained that this is how life works. We make choices based on what we believe. And if we have different information then we make different choices.

Then he spoke, again, about trusting God's plan and respecting the life path of others and, finally, of self-forgiveness. He had explained many times that the soul is eternal and that each soul had its own lessons that none of us are privy to knowing. I knew he was right. Ben wasn't gone; he had moved on to a new life. But I was not comforted by this.

"I think that if I had just done things differently, then he would not have found this life so painful." I cried from the agony of the guilt.

"You must stop berating yourself," Shiloh responded firmly. "You can no longer indulge yourself in self-loathing. It is holding you back from becoming who you are meant to be."

I took in both the meaning and the importance of his words.

"I hear you," I said.

"Good. Because what is to come is so important that you must not miss it."

I had no idea what he was talking about. But I was happy to let that sit. I knew he would not tell me. If all I needed to do to be ready for whatever was to come, was to love myself completely, that was challenge enough.

I did not know it then, but that conversation marked the last time that I agonized over Ben's death. I don't know how exactly he did it, but that last layer of guilt and shame dissolved, releasing me, allowing me to forgive myself. We never had to speak of it again.

It didn't take long for me to see that Shiloh's life was constant service. He focused entirely on God, and seeing his devotion, God asked him to do many things.

Once we were walking along the marina boardwalk, when he turned around to look behind us, and said quietly, "She fell."

I looked back to see what he was referring to, not startled at his usual hyperawareness of our surroundings. I saw an older woman on the ground about fifty feet away. Several people had stopped to help her up. We paused for a few moments, and then Shiloh said, "I'm not needed."

We walked on and I wondered, briefly, what he meant by his comment, but did not ask.

As he usually did, he responded to my unspoken question and said that when he sees someone in trouble he checks in with God, asking whether or not he is to help them.

"Why would God not want you to help?" I asked.

"God always wishes me to help," Shiloh replied, "but only God can decide what type of help someone needs."

We walked to a cafe and as we sat, each of us with a cup of peppermint tea, he spoke suddenly.

"I pray all the time," he said. "A constant prayer, in every moment."

I rarely asked Shiloh personal questions. I knew that if God deemed it helpful, then Shiloh would share whatever was important with me. But I could not help wondering what prayer it was, this constant prayer that he said. Once again, Shiloh answered me even though I had not spoken aloud.

"It is a wordless prayer. An attitude. If I had to put words to it, it is 'Yes, God, I'm listening'."

I knew Shiloh's service work was not easy. I realized quite quickly that he could feel every emotion that arose in me, and it was not a difficult leap of logic to understand that he experienced the emotions of others as well. I felt sure that it was deeply uncomfortable to be so aware of others' internal strife.

However, as he did for everyone, he willingly placed himself in the middle of the muck that was my self-experience so he could lead me out of it. As a result, I, who trusted no one, and who had been endlessly and repeatedly hurt by those closest to me, began to trust Shiloh.

Later that afternoon, after he had gone, I stood cleaning the galley on the boat. As often happened when I focused entirely on a meaningless task, inspiration struck.

I had a vision of Shiloh taking my hand and placing it into the enormously powerful hand of God. At that moment, the feeling that poured through me was not simply happiness. It was a deep knowing, a core knowing, of safety. Safety beyond the physical. Whatever happened, I was going to be okay. There is no safer place than resting in God's hand.

The next morning, after my routine of prayer and cleaning, I was ready for the day. I breathed for a few minutes, as Shiloh had advised, waiting to see whether God had any specific directions for me.

Instead, I had a sudden wave of deep sadness. I had spent all of my life, bumping into proverbial walls, suppressing my feelings, and careening from plan to plan and place to place hoping for some relief from the inner chaos.

Now that I had peace and an understanding of how God worked in my life, I felt profound anguish that I had wasted so much time not loving myself and not trusting the path that God set for me. I had squandered the most precious treasure in the Universe. I wished with all my heart that I had met Shiloh much sooner. What a waste of a life, to live in ignorance and lack of self-love.

I'm sure that the text I received from Shiloh a few minutes later was not a coincidence.

When I explained the deep sorrow that had overtaken me, he agreed that it is indeed quite difficult to know that we often prevent ourselves from living a beautiful life by holding a self-defeating perspective. Then he said that it is never too late to know who we are and to know who God is. Not even a deathbed realization of that truth is too late.

I was heartened by his words. Although I knew that life was not a certainty, I didn't think that my death would be that day. I could thoroughly enjoy this day, safe in God's care.

CHAPTER
SEVENTEEN

Y ou understand that you are not allowing your mother to heal, don't you?"

Shiloh's question surprised me. My mother and I had not spoken in several years. Our relationship had always been difficult but several years earlier, spurred by a particularly challenging interaction, I had let her know that I did not wish to interact with someone who treated me with such disregard. Not surprisingly, she had not responded.

I held other things against my mother, too. I held against her the fact that for four of my pre-pubertal years, one of my brothers had molested me, entering my room as I slept. Rightful or not, I had been angry she never noticed. When his actions came to light, years later, she didn't speak to me of it. I held that against her as well.

I had told Shiloh almost nothing of this. These and other stories had been fodder for many therapeutic sessions, and telling the tales had not helped me. Shiloh did not need to hear stories of my life to know what my wounds were. He focused not on examining events but on viewing my life from the perspective of my soul's journey.

With his question, he began a conversation that allowed me to move forward in a completely new way. Years earlier Shiloh had assured me that all that happened to me had a greater purpose than I had ever imagined. Now he wished to explain in detail the universal principles underpinning the guidance known as forgiveness.

It was not anything I said to my mother or my refusal to speak with her that harmed her. Rather, I held in place all that had happened. I was stunned to understand that forgiveness is not simply what we do when we want to be a good person. It is not a sign of goodness or a way to earn points to get into heaven. Both forgiveness and judgment have profound energetic consequences that Shiloh described in great detail. After his explanation, I understood the harmful effects of my lifetime of blaming those who I felt had hurt me.

Shiloh delivered this message while holding me in total

non-judgment making sure that I did not view myself harshly for the harm that I had surely caused. Like all unconscious mental habits, it was not easy to stop judging or blaming others even when I truly wished to do so.

I did not know that I would receive another lesson in complete forgiveness and non-judgment. I was going to strike out at Shiloh and he was going to forgive me entirely. But that was yet to come.

CHAPTER
EIGHTEEN

S hiloh had often said to me that if my focus is on God then that invites God into my life. But if I only speak to God during a specific moment in the day, then my focus is on human things. To truly live a divinely inspired life, he said, our focus should be on the Divine.

Later that year I moved to the country of Georgia where I lived in Batumi, renting a beautiful apartment that was a five-minute walk from the Black Sea. In Batumi, I was isolated by a language barrier. Because I had no one to speak to, it was easy to fill the time with God. I prayed as I walked. I prayed as I visited the aviary. I prayed as I sat on the balcony of the apartment, the sea to my left and the mountains to the right. I prayed as soon as I got up and just before

I went to bed in front of the small shrine I created on my bedside stand.

In early May, in a moment of quiet reflection before beginning my online work for the day, I knew that I wished to formalize my relationship with God.

I had been baptized as an infant, of course. But it had not been my choice. Now, I wanted to dedicate myself to God. I planned to wake early, just as the sun was rising and hopefully before anyone else was around.

I texted Shiloh of my intention.

"I'm sure it will be beautiful," he texted back. "When will you do it?"

"This weekend," I responded, happily.

The day of my self-dedication arrived, and when I stepped onto the wide strip of sand, two pigeons flew over my head and landed in front of me. Instead of flying off as I walked across the rock-strewn sand, they kept pace with me, a white dove on the left and a grey-black one on the right.

I walked into the cold water and submerged myself completely three times. "I, Sophia Rose, pledge myself to God."

Completely alone, I stayed in the water for a few minutes more and watched as the sun rose. Feeling happy and light, I crossed the sand on my way to the wide sidewalk. The prayer of gratitude that had become habitual while walking, came to mind. At that exact moment, just as I said the opening words, I looked down to take my next step. Lying in the sand, directly beneath my foot was a concrete paver in the shape of a cross. On it was etched a beautiful, intricately decorated, equal-armed cross. I gasped. I had not seen this paver in all the months I had been coming to this beach. How perfect that on this day, I had found it quite by accident.

A few days later, I walked around the old town of Batumi with no purpose except to escape the apartment. I happened upon a small bookstore that I had not seen before. I don't know why I stopped; I had no intention of buying a book. I had no room in my suitcase for books, and books in English are rather rare in Batumi, anyway. The store clerk approached me and greeted me in Russian, switching quickly to English at my halting response.

"Can I help you find something?"

I shook my head. "I'm just looking. Do you have books in English?"

She showed me a single round table, and right in the center was a small stack of a book I recognized—Jonathan Livingston Seagull. A new edition, it said, with a new ending. The cover of the book seemed to glow. I knew instantly

I would buy it. I had read it many years ago, but for some reason, it called to me.

The purchase was quite odd. I was not in the habit of reading. I had spent much of my life with my nose buried in a book, often reading six or seven in a week. It was a coping mechanism as real as any drug, but a few years earlier, I had finally curbed the addictive behavior. Now, I rarely read at all.

As soon as I returned to the apartment, I devoured the small book right away. Inexplicably, I cried the half hour it took to finish it. As I read the last chapter, the one newly added in this revised version, every hair on my body stood up. In the final sentences, I read that Jonathan Seagull returned once again to the flock and inspired a gull to find meaning in life. I cried copiously. I felt I was the gull and Shiloh had inspired me to live in a new and meaningful way.

As I closed the book, tears ran down my cheeks, and goosebumps covered every inch of me. I felt I was to write my experience of Shiloh. I could feel it so strongly that I jumped up and spun in place from the uncontainable knowing of it.

At that moment, the phone rang. In the circle where the avatar of the caller should be, it said King. I blinked and the word disappeared, leaving the initials SK.

I picked up the phone. It was unusual for Shiloh to call me without texting first. His timing was impeccable, as always.

"Hello," I said shakily, still reeling from what God had whispered in my heart.

"How are you, Sophia?"

I took a breath to steady myself. I hesitated trying to find the words.

"Shiloh, I just read a book that has moved me. Powerfully."

As soon as I finished those words, a rush of something that I cannot describe entered my body. It shot through me with such force that I doubled over. Then it happened again and again and again until I thought I might lose my grip on the Earth.

I gasped and tried to explain to Shiloh what had come over me, the rushing of inexplicably powerful energy. It did not abate, and I had trouble speaking.

"Something is happening—I can't explain." I gasped again. Then, I said what I needed to say. "Shiloh, I am supposed to tell others. About you. I'm so sure of it...," I gasped. "I can't explain..." I took another breath trying to steady myself within the strange current. "I just know it."

"Sophia, this feeling you have—it is your soul saying yes."

"Oh!" I gulped, effortfully. "It must be shouting 'YES' because this is so..." I gasped again, trying to get hold of myself. At any moment, I might either be turned inside out or I might fall to the ground. It was so powerful that I could scarcely tolerate it.

I hung up the phone, and eventually, the rushing current lessened and then subsided. I was elated. A message from God. The joy of it stayed with me a long while.

A few days later I had a vivid dream. I was in a Greek Orthodox church, sitting in an ornate wooden chair, when Shiloh entered the church and sat next to me. We sat quietly for a while and then he turned to me.

"I'm leaving. I've come to say goodbye."

I felt my heart contract. How could I manage without him?

"You will be fine," he said, and the reassurance and comfort that flowed through me at those words was indescribable. Then he hugged me and I could feel a perfect peace come over me. I knew he was right. All was well.

CHAPTER
NINETEEN

I had been in Georgia for seven months when one morning for no reason in particular, I felt it was time to leave.
Within a few hours my bag was packed and the next day I
boarded a flight to the UK through Kyiv, where I spent the
night in the airport.

Before I left Shiloh wished me a safe journey, suggesting
that I ask God to smooth my travels. His reminder was
well-timed. I had been rushing to get ready to leave and
had not taken the time to ask God to bless my journey.
As I waited for the taxi, I asked for divine intervention
along the way. *God, please be with me on this journey.*
Please find a safe place for me to rest overnight. Please, oh
please, find me a flat place to lie down. I had spent nights

in airports before. Invariably, they were highly uncomfortable and sleepless.

I arrived in Kyiv at midnight and proceeded to the gate where my connecting flight was to depart the next morning. It was empty, of course. I settled in a chair and prepared for a long wait.

Within half an hour, a group of young men came and sat across from me. Before long, their rowdiness forced me out of my chosen spot, and I walked down the large, bright corridor to the very end of the concourse. I turned and crossed to the other side of the wide hallway where I noticed a darkened area on my left. No moving screens blaring messages, no lights, no chairs. Only empty space.

Mentally I thanked those boys who had sat across from me. They nudged me out of my chair into a much better spot. I settled against the wall in the darkened area and tucked my backpack under my arm. Then I drew up my knees and rested my forehead on them.

I awoke when someone touched my shoulder. My loud indrawn gasp of shock surprised the uniformed woman who leaned over me. I saw her take a step back and say something in Russian. I blinked, confused.

She traced a rectangle in the air. My ticket. She wanted my ticket.

I dug it out and handed it to her. She said something else and then began to walk off, my ticket in hand.

I was indignant. Why take my ticket? Right then, I noticed the full moon framed in the wall of windows. Something about its constancy was reassuring. I said to myself what Shiloh had repeated many times—trust that all is well. I took a deep breath. My irritation subsided and I waited for whatever was to happen.

Within five minutes the uniformed woman was back, motioning for me to follow her. After a few minutes of trailing her, mystified, through the airport, she stopped and opened a door. Then she motioned me through the doorway, standing aside, a pleased smile on her face.

It was a nice-sized room. A table with four chairs. A microwave. A sink. And a large window to the outside through which the full moon shone. Best of all, an enormous couch took up the length of one wall. It was the perfect place to stretch out fully and sleep.

She handed my ticket back to me. I realized then that she only asked for it to see how long it would be before my flight. I smiled gratefully and she shut the door, still smiling.

God had arranged a flat place for me to rest, just as I had asked.

Once back on the boat, I unpacked and settled into a routine. I was less isolated, attending ballet classes and forging new acquaintances. However, it was difficult to maintain a prayerful existence when nothing around me was prayerful. Further, I was quite busy with work and the distractions conspired to draw me away from devotion.

One afternoon, a few weeks after I arrived, I stood in the galley washing up after lunch. I don't know what made me look up, but staring at me through the porthole was a seagull. Its yellow eye regarded me, unblinking. I stared at him for a long while. He didn't move and I considered the strangeness of it. I had been on and off this boat for nearly two years and no gull had ever looked through the porthole at me.

Just then the gull took flight. But it didn't go far. It landed on the boat's hatch and began pecking at it forcefully. The sound ricocheted like gunshots. I leaped from the boat onto the pontoon, waving my arms. The startled gull flew away.

Shiloh had told me many times that everything brings a message from the Divine. I stood there a moment, wondering what the message was. I waited, trusting that God had something to show me.

Suddenly, I had it. A seagull was pounding on the hatch

that opened to the sky. The symbolism was quite clear—a message from above. Directly below the hatch was where I had stored my suitcase. In that suitcase was the Jonathan Livingston Seagull book. Though the rest of the suitcase was emptied long ago, I had failed to unpack it.

I pulled the book out immediately and placed it on the display shelf remembering that I had been asked to write about Shiloh. With chagrin, I realized I had received that message but had not acted on it. I must do so. This was not something to save for another time, but now.

I sat down and began to write, beginning with how I had met Shiloh. I was astonished to recall that time in Egypt. I was so different from that person standing lost and bitter at the edge of the water.

Within a few months, I was on the move again, nudged out of the comfortable boat by visa restrictions. From the balcony of my hotel on a small island in the Cyclades, I could see two white churches, each with a spire and a blue-painted dome.

I walked to the larger of the two chapels in the early morning. As I climbed the last flight of steep steps, a man exited a small door in a low building adjacent to the chapel.

He looked up at me, surprised to see a tourist in the off-season. After exchanging the usual pleasantries, he asked where I was from.

"The USA," I said. "But I haven't been there in several years."

"Where do you live, then?" he asked.

I shrugged. "Wherever."

"How long will you stay here?"

"I don't know."

He considered me closely, his head to one side. "So, where will you go next?" he finally asked.

I shook my head and lifted one shoulder, smiling.

His response was resentful. "You are living the life I want to live."

I understood. I had stood in his shoes for most of my life. I remained silent.

The man came to his senses and withdrew the anger he had initially directed at me. Instead, he cast about for something else to blame.

"In my work, I cannot travel. It is not possible."

I nodded. I could not malign the shoes I had stood in, not so many years prior. I did not tell him what Shiloh had taught me. That when we ask God for help, we can be free of the trap of victimhood.

Instead, I held up my hand to say goodbye and went into

the church to deposit a coin and light a candle in gratitude for my life filled with the hard lessons that had brought me to this point. And, of course, deep gratitude to God for sending Shiloh to show me the way to Him.

CHAPTER
TWENTY

When my children were teenagers, foot pain prevented me from running the distances I was otherwise capable of. No matter the shoes, my feet could not handle the pounding and I eventually abandoned running. More recently, any walk farther than a few miles resulted in pain.

One evening I was sitting in a restaurant with my son when he came to visit me in England, and it felt as though shards of glass were poking up through my shoes. My son saw me wincing.

"What is the problem?" he asked.

"I don't know. But any time I walk more than a few miles, they hurt badly."

"We haven't walked a few miles today, Mom. We've hardly walked at all."

He was right. My feet hurt terribly for no reason.

"What does Shiloh say?" he asked.

"Shiloh says what he always says about my feet. That the pain means I do not trust I am supported in my life."

Trust. Shiloh had spoken of it many times. When I fully trusted God to support me in all ways, he said, my life would change radically. But, to my extreme chagrin, distrust was deeply ingrained.

One day, though, several years after meeting Shiloh, I realized that my feet didn't hurt. Further, I could not recall the last time they had pained me.

I texted Shiloh. "Do you recall that I used to complain about my feet all the time?"

"Yes," he replied.

"I can't remember when they last hurt."

"That is wonderful, Sophia. Healing is a beautiful process. You have done a lot of work in learning to trust God."

As usual, Shiloh took no credit. But I knew that it was through his hand that God brought this and many other healings.

After a few months in Greece, I returned to the States for the summer and while I was there, I developed a toothache. Although I wished to wait until I was back in the UK for treatment, after several weeks the tooth ached so badly that it kept me awake at night. The pain extended from my lower jaw, up the side of my head, and pounded in the temple. Chewing solid food became impossible and soon I began subsisting on yogurt and smoothies. From my training in immunology, I understood how an infection is processed by the body and that infections in the head should be addressed. If ignored, they can travel to the brain or cause sepsis.

Reluctantly, I went to a local dentist who confirmed the presence of an abscess and gave me a prescription for antibiotics. He also said that the tooth was cracked to the root and needed to be extracted. For several reasons including a family history of Crohn's, I stubbornly avoided antibiotics. I decided not to fill the prescription but made an appointment the next week to have the tooth removed.

That night I spoke to Shiloh for about ten minutes telling him how upset I was that the molar needed to come out. Eight of my teeth had been pulled for orthodontic reasons, and I didn't feel I had any to spare. When I finished describing the situation, he said that perhaps my upset indicated that I wasn't ready for it to be removed.

I was in agony, though, and I could not imagine continuing

to live with an abscess that could cause serious problems if unaddressed. I went to bed steeling myself to endure the pain over the next few days before the extraction. The next morning, I woke up, ate breakfast, and started to work. Then, it hit me. My tooth didn't hurt. Not one bit. Not at all. I had no idea what to think. I had spoken to Shiloh just before I had gone to bed and then I awoke, pain-free.

I called Shiloh. "Did you heal my toothache?"

He admitted that as we spoke he had looked deeply into the reason for the infection. He could see how it was linked to an aspect of my subconscious relating to my mother. In his remarkably understated way, he said that often when he focuses on things, they resolve. Despite his humble manner, the fact remained that he had focused on the infection and within hours, it had disappeared.

The analytical part of my mind was flummoxed. I knew that for an abscess to disappear entirely, the pus needed to go somewhere. I could not imagine that it could be absorbed that quickly or that it had exited through the skin given there was no exit wound nor was there a discharge. But the part of me that knew Shiloh was a man of God was not surprised in the least.

I thought no more about that tooth except to marvel that it no longer hurt. Six months later, however, when I was in a cafe in the UK, I bit down on something quite hard and I felt a twinge of pain. For the next three weeks, I experienced discomfort as the infection returned. I contemplated the situation, wondering as to my best course of action.

Then, I had a strange dream. I was brushing my teeth and the tooth fell out into the sink. In the dream, I was incredibly pleased and I held it in my hand regarding it with great fondness and gratitude.

I pondered that dream. Losing the tooth felt like a resolution, as though I were letting go of a part of myself, my past, that I no longer needed. The tooth was full of mercury amalgam and from a physical perspective that is likely why it had cracked. Instead of thinking of it as a failure or a loss, I saw it as a release from a broken, toxic part of me. I felt at peace with it. I was ready for the extraction.

I truly have no real understanding of how Shiloh healed an abscess overnight, simply by focusing on it but that is what happened.

I often exercised on the boat, doing yoga when the water was calm. One morning, I was in an arm balance and for no reason, I fell out of the position. Instead of falling backward onto my feet, I fell strangely forward and the entire weight of my body crashed down onto my forearm, bending my wrist in a way that it should never bend. The pain was so intense my stomach heaved. Thankfully, it was quite empty.

After the initial shock subsided, I leaped from the boat onto the pontoon and plunged my arm as far into the icy water as far as it would go until I could not feel my hand. Then I went back onto the boat. When the cold dissipated, the pain in my wrist was excruciating. I repeated the icy water plunge several times.

After an hour, I curled my arm across my chest. My hand was completely useless. That night, getting undressed for bed was incredibly difficult. I am quite right-handed and life became astonishingly difficult. Even holding something as light as the bedsheet was suddenly challenging.

The next day was no better. Fixing my hair in its usual bun, tying my shoes—impossible. With my right forearm resting against my chest, I braced myself to deal with one-handed life. I walked to the store in the marina with the laces on my shoes flopping and purchased a pair of soft boots that I could pull on with one hand.

When I returned to the boat, Shiloh texted me with his usual incredible timing. "How are you, Sophia?"

I told him of my injury and the impossibility of using my hand for anything.

He asked me several questions about the location of the

pain and then said that I should place my palm as flat as possible and just let it be supported.

I uncurled my hand from its safe place on my chest and placed it, gingerly, on the cushion next to me, spreading my fingers as much as possible. After a minute, he said he didn't believe there to be any broken bones. Just let it rest for a while, he advised.

To my surprise, I yawned widely. I was incredibly sleepy and the urge to nap was overwhelming.

As soon as I hung up, I fell asleep exactly where I was sitting, chin on chest. I awoke half an hour later, startled that I had fallen so soundly asleep in the middle of the day. I stood and walked to the door, which I opened. When I stepped up into the wheelhouse, the sun was shining brightly.

Suddenly, I froze. I had used my right hand to open the door. The hand that had been completely unusable not half an hour before was completely pain-free and perfectly functional.

I texted Shiloh. "I can use my hand! It doesn't hurt!"

He replied that he could see that it was healing as he spoke with me but that the mind sometimes can't accept healing. Sleep allows a more receptive state, he said.

I was awed and grateful, though, I knew him too well by then to be surprised.

Over the years that I have known Shiloh, I noticed some other unusual aspects of being near him. Once my back hurt for about four months, for a reason that took me quite a while to work out and deal with. One particularly difficult morning I sat with a pillow at my back trying to work. The pain was so intense that concentrating was difficult. Shiloh called and we spoke for a short while. I didn't mention my back—I felt it was mine to address.

After we hung up, I began to work again. It was not until I stood to make myself a cup of tea that I realized my back didn't hurt at all. The next day the pain returned. Over the next few months, each time I spoke with Shiloh the pain would disappear and then later would return, almost like what he offered would wear off in his absence. Although I eventually discovered the reason for the back ache, speaking with Shiloh provided obvious relief, as though he reminded me of what it felt like to be well and whole.

One day while squatting for hours weeding the garden, my hip dislocated partially. Dislocations of the jaw, hip, and knee had been a common theme in my young life, the first occurring when I was not yet two years old. But it had been many years since my hip had done such a thing. The pain of a partial dislocation of the hip was notable. But it was moving from a sitting position to a standing position that was sharply agonizing. When you live alone, however, you just deal with whatever arises. I discovered I could walk reasonably well once I aligned my body correctly over the hip but I avoided the transition from sitting to standing as much as possible.

The day after it happened, I was propped carefully on the couch, with a candle and meditative music in quiet observation of the hip and its message to me, whatever it was. I had not moved for most of the morning, hoping to avoid the sharp pain that accompanied standing up. Then Shiloh called. We did not speak of the hip, but of other more interesting matters concerning God's relationship with humanity. As Shiloh spoke, without thinking, I rose from the couch and walked to the window, listening carefully to his words. At that moment, a deer bounded joyfully across the lawn and I gasped in delight. Then, I suddenly realized that I had stood and walked to the window entirely without pain. Shiloh had not needed to focus on my hip. Healing occurred simply by listening to him.

This pattern—discomfort that disappeared when speaking with Shiloh—repeated so many times over the years that I almost forgot how remarkable it was.

Shiloh's gifts are not limited to healing. Once I showed him a photograph of some friends and quite immediately, he summarized succinctly and accurately, who they were, though I had never spoken to him of them. But it was not simply pictures that held information. If I spoke to Shiloh about another person, he knew their motivations, personalities, and wounds. I do not pretend to understand how he was able to do this.

Once I told him in passing that I had the idea to ask one of my clients to assign me a new project. Immediately, Shiloh said that it was important that I act quickly, stressing that time was of the essence. Then he said that the situation with the client was time-sensitive because the company was undergoing a reorganization and that I needed to let them know of my interest. By now, I knew Shiloh well enough to take everything he said quite seriously. I heeded his advice and within a few days had a conversation with my client whose first words were that my email had been quite timely because they were undergoing a reorganization. She assured me my proposal would be placed into the mix. Shiloh's advice was stunningly accurate in both timing and substance.

I cannot dismiss Shiloh's insights as coincidence or even intuition. I saw repeatedly over several years that he knew things about me, about others, and even world events that were incredibly accurate. I do not recall them all chiefly because there are so many. But he consistently knows things that he can have no conventional way of knowing.

I t was the end of my third summer on the boat when I called Shiloh for advice about a physical issue I could not clear. Despite years of daily yoga, my right shoulder was hurting and the ache radiated to my neck. The persistent pain and restriction were beginning to affect my movements. I knew if I did not heed the message that my body sent me, the message would become more insistent, more painful. I had tried my best but I had not been able to shift it.

"Sophia, I see your shoulder carries a burden that you do not need to carry."

"A burden? What burden?" I was mystified.

"It is not a thing," he said. "It is more of an attitude toward people in your life." He said my strong mothering instinct drew people to me who wished to be cared for. But their welfare was not my responsibility.

I was troubled by the idea that my deepest caregiving instincts were a problem. I had become a teacher because I loved children and caring for them had been a great joy for me.

"I feel confused. I shouldn't care about others?"

But that was not what he was saying. He explained that people needed to establish their own connection to God, asking for and receiving God's perfect help. If they look to a person rather than God, he said, it is not good for them and it is not good for the person.

"But you are helping *me*," I pointed out.

"Sophia, God brings people to me to be healed who have asked for healing. I do not take responsibility for their healing."

Shiloh stressed that only God had the full picture. I must allow God to guide all of my actions.

One week later, I awoke suddenly and completely at 2:30 in the morning. I lay looking up at the blank ceiling in Sirius's bow, wide awake. Astonished, I saw before my eyes words in thick, flaming letters. A fiery sentence flickered across the white ceiling as though alive. I read it several times before it disappeared.

"Thou art much weaker than thou art able to comprehend."

Despite the awesome glow, the feeling behind those words made my heart soar. There was not a single shred of judgment—just a blast of unconditional love, bliss, and joy that is the signature of God.

Along with that flood of God's love came the insight into exactly what those words meant for me. Compared to the mind of God, my mind is incredibly weak. No idea that I have ever had or could ever have, approaches the magnificence of God. Placing trust in my thoughts or in human things was folly. I must fully surrender to God.

The message was so clear and so beautiful that I began to cry and laugh with joy at the same time. It was quite similar to what Shiloh had told me the week before, and I realized this must be a truly important message for it to be delivered twice in such a short period.

God was in charge. And He wanted to be sure that I knew it.

CHAPTER
TWENTY-TWO

O ne evening while on the boat, I received a text from
Shiloh.

"How are you this evening, Sophia? Do you have time
for a chat?"

Whenever Shiloh texted, I put all else aside. It meant he
had something to say, for he never called to amuse himself
or pass the time. Polite as always, Shiloh asked me how
I was and we spoke for a few minutes about how things
were going for me. Then he asked me if I would check
the engine bay. Shiloh had an uncanny knack for knowing
when Sirius needed attention. When I checked, there was
indeed a new oil stain growing. He commented that the
engine likely needed to be serviced soon, and I made a
mental note to look for a mechanic to perform the service.

"How are you, in yourself?" he asked. He often asked this, particularly if we had spoken of mundane issues, to bring the conversation to what was truly important.

I don't recall what specific frustration I spoke of. It was likely the usual issues that arose to show me that I lacked full trust in the process of my life as guided by God. I knew by now that this was my life lesson—giving up control.

Gently, without reprimand, without accusation, without frustration, Shiloh spoke of what it looked like to trust. He talked of God's laws and how they worked not just in my life but in everyone's. He spoke of the eternity of those laws. It is impossible to accurately repeat what he said in that hour-long call, but as he spoke, I had that feeling that always came over me when Shiloh spoke of God and the laws He had set in place. What he said felt so beautiful, so hopeful, so full of love for all, that I was suffused with profound contentment. All felt right with the world.

I vividly recall lying down that evening with a smile, resting in a glow of safety, as though God's hands were cupping me gently.

The next morning when I awoke, I lay there. I saw the sun streaming in through the porthole. I heard gulls calling. I breathed, completely content. I had no thoughts about myself or the coming day or about yesterday. No thought at all. Just that same feeling of deep well-being that had suffused me while listening to Shiloh the evening before.

All of a sudden, I was between. How can I describe what is logically impossible? I felt as though I had slipped out of time, in between one minute and the next. I could almost see the structure of time superimposed artificially onto the greater truth of eternity.

With a great clarity, I could feel the air. Not the air in the boat but all of the air. It was alive with a powerful and ancient consciousness. The air was aware of itself and it was aware of me and all living things. From inside the boat, I could see the living air flowing over the water. The water, too, was a separate consciousness, equally ancient and aware of its importance in all of life on Earth. I did not see with my eyes but with a sense that I did not recognize, one that merged seeing and feeling into a single sensation. A pine tree grew near the berth, and although I could not see the tree from inside the boat, I sensed every part of that pine tree—its needles, its roots, its bark, and the sap that flowed within. I felt the pine tree connected to the water and to the air and to me.

The feeling of stepping out of time into this infinite knowingness of Life was pure bliss. Joy. The incredible truth of the infinite, interwoven, and sacred nature of life. I was hyperaware of myself and my body. Each breath was a lifetime.

Then I did the thing that popped me out of this blissful

experience of life as it really is. I had a thought. *This must be what Shiloh knows.*

Instantly, I was catapulted from a blissful feeling of infinite love and life, back into my limited mind. Because I tried to label the experience, categorize it, and think of it as *something*, I lost it.

I finally understood why Shiloh endlessly advised me not to judge anything. Not to make a story about anything. Not to describe anything. To understand this world, I must simply experience it.

The night before the unusual experience I had spoken with Shiloh and our conversation had engendered a feeling of peaceful contentment that was profoundly calming. That feeling was still with me when I awoke. I could not help but wonder whether that sensation inspired the onset of the unusual feeling of timelessness.

When I told Shiloh of the unusual episode, he said that when we simply feel, shutting our minds off, we can understand things that lie beneath the surface. We can get beyond what our eyes can see.

This experience opened my eyes to how differently Shiloh moves in the world. I had seen how he was able to sense more than I could, always extremely aware of things that I did not notice. It is why he knew the old woman fell when he could not have seen it happen—he felt it. It is how he saw into people's hearts and minds and not only those standing in front of him.

This ability was why, when he bought Sirius, he was able to see how to fix her engine without touching it. The inspector had condemned the engine and had told Shiloh it needed to be replaced. But he sat next to the engine and felt the single part that needed to be changed to bring her back to life. Another time, I splashed some diesel as I filled Sirius' tank and it got all over my hands and face. He was hours away from Sirius but he knew. He asked me if all was well, saying he smelled the diesel.

That blissful experience of timelessness has never returned to me. I cannot sense the air and the water in the way that I did in those few seconds. But the experience opened my eyes to how limited my mind is. And showed me how thoroughly Shiloh had mastered his.

CHAPTER
TWENTY-THREE

In the nearly four years since meeting Shiloh, he had been nothing but patient and kind, freely sharing guidance and time. But I, who had a life populated largely with people who pretended to care for me while doing the opposite, carried the scars of those experiences. And those scars hindered me greatly.

One day, during a phone call that otherwise was unremarkable, Shiloh described something he had done the prior month. But he had forgotten he had told me about it already. I listened again, and this time, the details sounded different. I thought nothing of it as he spoke, but after we hung up, I began to consider what it meant.

For two hours, my heart beat faster than usual. My mind turned the two descriptions over and over.

Although Shiloh's minor comment had nothing to do with me, and the perceived discrepancy was minor, it sparked the old worry that people were not what they seemed. My tendency to distrust everyone and everything mushroomed out of control.

I didn't want to ask Shiloh about the differences between the two descriptions of the event. But I knew that if I didn't, he would sense my doubt, such was his sensitivity.

I called Shiloh. I explained that he had told me two different things and that I wondered why. Without comment on my doubt, he repeated the two things that he had said about his experience clearly, side by side. As he did so, I saw no difference, only two sides of the same coin. On top of it, I had misinterpreted what he said.

Then he addressed the real problem, deep inside me. I needed to let go of my past experiences, he said, so I could see the truth of the present. I was so poised for untruth that I found it, even when it did not exist. He spoke for a long while about how people project their ideas onto others and the ill effects of that projection.

Then, for nearly an hour, he spoke of how to discern others, to discern the truth of any situation, and the different ways we can be derailed in attempts to know the truth. It is impossible to repeat his words here with any accuracy, and I do not pretend to recall all that he said. But when we hung up it felt almost like little bubbles of joy were bursting in my heart. This is how I knew to trust him. Truth has a resonance and when you feel it, it is quite an unmistakably beautiful thing.

Sometimes I wondered why Shiloh continued to speak to me. I doubted him, I was a slow learner, and I seemed to need to hear the same things over and over. I was grateful that he didn't give up on me.

The next day, as I walked the half hour to an exercise class, I felt light and happy. Shiloh was exactly who I had thought he was—a man of God who had no agenda other than to offer healing. His faith and connection to God were such that I could trust him, even when my understanding was flawed.

The yoga class that I attended on that December day was difficult. It pushed me to the edge of my physical ability and stamina. It was wonderful to know that I was stronger than I imagined and I enjoyed the feeling as I walked home slowly along the beach. I eventually stopped to face the choppy waters of the channel, basking in the soft rain and sea spray. I stood for a long while feeling grateful for my life and thanking God for all I had been given. Before I turned from the water, I said something that I did not typically say.

I'm listening, God, if there's anything I need to hear.

I waited a few minutes but heard nothing. Deeply peaceful, I turned to leave, but before my foot could even hit the ground, I heard God.

The message was as though a deep vibration sang through my body bringing with it profound love and clarity and light.

"I HAVE CHOSEN SHILOH; YOU ARE NOT TO QUESTION HIM."

The statement and the utter joy that is God resounded through my body, my mind, and deep into my soul. I understood unequivocally that Shiloh speaks with God's authority.

Words cannot adequately capture the magnificent feeling accompanying this message. Despite the clear reprimand that God's words contained, I was elated. I knew without a doubt I was perfectly loved. Nothing I could do could cause me to lose God's unconditional love.

However, I had questioned God's chosen messenger, and He let me know with stunning clarity that this was not appropriate. His correction was delivered in such a way that instead of shame or fear, I felt nothing but deepest gratitude and joy.

CHAPTER
TWENTY-FOUR

Despite the wonderful experiences and divine messages, the winter months that followed God's declaration were extremely difficult. More challenging, even, than when Ben died.

Every few weeks, I dropped into a deep depression, often accompanied by much self-castigation. I, who had been offered so much by way of healing, could not forgive myself for being depressed each time the huge weight descended on me. After several cycles of low mood and then recovery, I began to wish, intensely, for release from the agony of the roller coaster.

Shiloh kept in close touch. He knew the dark place I was in.

Depression often made me feel that my life was awful, but it wasn't true. Whenever he spoke to me, I could recall that I enjoyed and craved the peaceful solitude. Each time, with just a brief conversation he reminded me of the perfection of whatever God brought to me, and with that, I could easily return to a peaceful state.

I woke up one day after several weeks of peace and for some reason on that morning, I realized that it had been weeks since anyone had asked me how I was. Weeks since I had a real conversation or a kind word from anyone who knew my name. I tried to fight my way out of it, using the methods that Shiloh had shown me.

On that particularly difficult day, I decided to walk the half hour into town along the sea wall to attempt to leave behind the black mood. As I walked, I prayed desperately. *God, please be with me. I need to feel your presence.* I imagined myself walking hand-in-hand with God down the sidewalk. Usually, it was enough to deliver me from my depressed state, but not today. I devolved into a repetitive begging to keep myself from breaking down on the sidewalk. *Help me. Help me. Help me.*

I started to say it out loud. "Help me, help me." I didn't care what anyone thought.

Eventually, I ended up at a roundabout with a statue and a fountain in the middle, a popular place for people and pigeons to lunch. I sat on the grass near the pavement that circled the fountain and stared up at the clouds in the sky, trying to keep the tears at bay.

Within a few minutes, a small van pulled up about fifteen feet to my left. The driver had pulled directly onto the circular pavement—a pedestrian area. I was irritated at his disregard for the usual division between pedestrians and vehicles.

A man jumped from the driver's seat and slid open the side door of the van. Within minutes, he extended a small awning from the roof of the van and placed a few chairs beneath it. It wasn't until he arranged a tall banner on its stand, and the sign sprang straight into the air that I could see what he was about. This was a portable church and he was a minister.

My jaw dropped and my skin tingled. I had just begged God for half an hour to show me that he was with me and a portable church appeared next to me, mere feet from where I sat on the grass.

I laughed in delight at the quick answer to my prayer. I did not speak to the minister — I had received the message from God directly. He said, "I am everywhere. But if you need proof here is a sign that says so."

Just then, in that moment of astonishment, a gigantic white feather fell from the sky. Not in a floaty, feathery way, but straight down like an arrow and it stuck into the ground directly in front of me. An exclamation point delivered by one of God's creatures.

It was exactly what I needed to see. I was not alone.

Unfortunately, the message that I was not alone was not the grand turning point I had hoped. Over the long winter, I vacillated between joy and depression. Shiloh spoke to me many times of God's perfect love for me. His words shifted me to a place of surrender and joy, and I was content and at peace for weeks. Then, suddenly, I would fall back into a deep hole again.

One night, I lay in the bow of the boat staring at the ceiling, long into the night. The desire to be done with the unending struggle was so intense that I could think of no reason to endure the agony. I thought of several ways to end my life, each easier than the last. I understood Ben perfectly. The thought that I could go and be with him in a better place was more than tempting.

That night, the pain in my head was overwhelming and I felt my skull might split in two. After several hours of agony, I decided to end it. Desperately I shouted, "This is it. I'm going to do it."

In the silence that echoed, I heard a voice. "Whatever you decide is fine."

The voice was one of perfect acceptance
tional love. It was Shiloh's voice.

Instantly, upon connecting with the reality of ᴗ
unconditional love for me no matter my choices, I was
aligned with the deepest truth of myself, and that truth was
that my soul was here for a purpose. The effect of that align-
ment was so instantaneous that every bit of agony that had
been ripping me apart was entirely gone. I fell into a deeply
peaceful sleep.

The next morning when I awoke, I knew that no matter
how bad I felt I would never, ever take my own life. I had
been faced with a terrible decision and I had found that deep
in my soul I wanted life. It was something I had needed to
discover.

I told Shiloh what happened, of course. "Shiloh, it is so hard
to believe that I let negative thoughts get the better of me."

He understood the difficulties that I endured. His advice
was practical and inspiring. "Just remember that if a thought
is not loving, we must reject it. Because God is love."

His words lifted me as they always did. Then he spoke
specifically of my frustration at the repeated cycling between
depression and joy, saying that we lived in a difficult world.

"It does not matter how many times we fall away, Sophia.
The important thing is to seek God."

CHAPTER
TWENTY-FIVE

Though that winter was my darkest, it was also my lightest. One particularly lovely day was filled with nothing remarkable except a feeling of deep contentment. The day sparkled for no reason except that I felt loved by God. That afternoon I stood in the galley amid the fairy lights and the aroma of a scented candle, contemplating how lucky I was to be in such a space.

In that silent moment, I received another divine message delivered clearly into the calmness of my mind.

"Shiloh will tell you things that are hard to hear. You must listen."

I recognized the feeling of God's unconditional love. I was overjoyed at another message from Him.

Shiloh must indeed have something crucial to tell me for God to point it out in advance. I overflowed with joy and certainty that I could hear anything that needed to be said. I felt strong, knowing that whatever Shiloh had to say would be for my highest good. I hugged the message to me, happily, though it was cautionary.

A few days later, depression struck again. In my suffering, I messaged Shiloh, confused as to how easily I could be knocked off my faith path.

Shiloh explained that those who wish to serve God often have challenging lives. I knew he was right. I would never have embarked on this journey to faith if it had not been for the death of my son.

He told me that when things are truly painful the most beautiful thing I could do is surrender all of it to God. I was buoyed once again, though I knew that to experience agony and to voluntarily accept it and give it to God is a difficult thing. My first reaction when upsetting things happen is to run away.

My second is to attack.

Not long afterward, when it was quite cold and wintry, Shiloh came to Sirius to check on her. He was much thinner than I had ever seen and he shivered in the chilly air. This was not the Shiloh I knew who effortlessly withstood the coldest of winds in his shirtsleeves. He appeared tired and when he spoke his voice rasped.

Though he rarely spoke of the specifics of his life path, he acknowledged it was a difficult time.

"So many people judge me. So many people receive the healing I have to offer but then do not acknowledge it."

I could see he was tired. Exhausted, even.

"I wonder if I will be able to do what God sent me here for," he said.

I was quiet, not wishing to pry. He did not complain or lament but simply shared the truth of the moment.

We went on to speak of other things including repairs on Sirius, that had been languishing.

Not long after Shiloh's visit, we spoke on the phone. I wondered about changing my job and my location, thinking my continued unhappiness was a sign to leave or a need to change my life radically.

"I keep thinking that I should go back to teaching," I said, in testament to how unhappy I was. It had been nearly five years since I stepped foot in a classroom.

n speaking of jobs and living situations, which

n concerns, Shiloh spoke of giving up control

to God. He went on to repeat the things I had heard often: how important it was to listen to God in each moment, to surrender the processes of my life to God, to see the messages that my life reflected to me.

Then he said, "Do you not see that Sirius is rotting?"

I sucked in my breath. It was true. I had not paid enough attention to the canvas that covered the boat and during a six-month absence, water had seeped in and damaged the boat to the point that boards were rotting. Further, the strakes along the outside of the boat were beginning to show severe weathering and if nothing were done, they would rot as well.

"Everything around us is a reflection of ourselves," he said.

I cringed at the truth of that statement. If the boat was rotting around me, then I was rotting too. I was not caring well enough for Sirius or myself.

"What happened, Sophia? What has happened to your faith?" he asked.

I was trying! Couldn't he see I was trying? In that moment, I did what I always do when I am backed into a corner by a truth from which there is no escape. I struck out in anger.

"I could ask you the same," I said.

"What?" he asked.

I said nothing, not wishing to repeat that which was so clearly a specious attack.

Shiloh broke the silence that followed with a forthright statement that was neither distressed nor calm, but something in between. "I think we should continue this conversation later." And he hung up.

Sickened, I stood up and pulled out my suitcase from its well-hidden position in the bow. I began to pack. I was a failure on this spiritual journey, and I had attacked my mentor when he told me the truth about myself.

I had turned on the one person who had truly tried to help me, who had displayed endless forbearance and patience.

What's worse, God had warned me. Not just once but three times. He had told me that he had chosen Shiloh and not to question him; He told me how little I knew, in flaming letters, because regular letters would not suffice; and He had specifically said that Shiloh would say something difficult to hear and that I must listen. Instead, I lashed out.

I had failed God. Now I would be, justifiably, cast out.

I did not have many things. I had nearly finished packing my clothes when the phone rang fifteen minutes later. It was Shiloh.

I dreaded answering it, dreaded to hear what he would say. I was sure he would tell me that he could no longer be my spiritual mentor.

"Sophia, I have asked God to re-align all that has happened this day to the perfection of His will."

Then he reminded me, gently, that his relationship with God is not something that others may comment on.

But I was not willing to receive the stunning lesson in forgiveness and non-judgment that he had just given me.

"Shiloh, God warned me. He told me you would say something hard to hear and that I must listen. But I didn't." The sickness in my heart was overwhelming. There is no worse feeling than knowing that God asked something of you, only to find that you were not capable of it.

"I have failed God," I said, miserably.

Shiloh would not join me in my self-punishment. "God does not blame or reject or vilify or seek vengeance. And neither can we, if we wish to live in God's realm."

After I intentionally lashed out at him, he never spoke of it. He forgave me so entirely that I never detected a single moment of hesitation when he spoke with me nor any difference in the way he treated me. I asked him how he was able to do this so completely, without hesitation.

"I just handed it to God," he said.

It was a stunning display of the power of surrender to God. To this day, I am sure that Shiloh holds not a shred of blame or anger, though I certainly struck him with my words.

CHAPTER
TWENTY-SIX

The day began, quite benignly, with a text from Shiloh.

"How are you feeling, Sophia?"

"I'm fine, Shiloh," I replied, not knowing how completely untrue that statement was. The long winter was over and I had spent a pleasant spring and summer traveling. Now that I was back on Sirius, I was unaware it was time for a vast and profound clearing.

Much later, after it was all over, Shiloh told me he knew it was coming. That he had sensed it rising even before God explicitly warned him.

That morning in late August, I swept the boat. I had my morning tea, and I was about to check my email to see whether I had received the green light on a freelance writing job that had been, quite aggravatingly, delayed for a fourth week. Instead, I sent another text to Shiloh.

"I was thinking of getting a massage," I said. I hadn't had a massage in many years.

"Nice," he replied. "A massage can clear trauma."

His comment about clearing trauma seemed somewhat inconsequential. But on this day, for whatever reason, the benign statement snapped something in me. A dam burst and what came flying out was irrepressible chaos.

An enormous rush of anger, red hot rage, filled me. I had no idea why but there was no time to analyze it before it took me over. I began screaming and crying and throwing whatever came to hand. Finally, I hurled myself onto the floor, beating my fists against the wood and gasping for air.

Rage was quickly replaced with other equally incomprehensible emotions, jumbled together.

Fear. Powerlessness. Frustration.

Terror. Revulsion. Hatred.

Shame. Self-loathing. Nausea.

A ceaseless, unstoppable buffeting of unbearable emotions. Most unbearable, though, was the confusion. What was this?

Eventually, I climbed into the berth. I lay in agony, my face turned to the wall. I neither ate nor slept. My misery was so acute that I began imagining all the places where I could hurt myself and not die. I longed for physical pain, for blood. I became obsessed with the single knife that I owned. I did not move from where I lay for almost two days.

Finally, weak and dehydrated, I dragged myself from the berth. I drank water. After changing into my swimsuit, I walked slowly to the ocean where I submerged myself over and over until I could feel a lessening of the self-loathing, the terror, the anger. After an hour or so I sat in the sun, gathering strength for the walk back. I was still shaken, but at least I was not raging.

When I returned to the boat, I texted Shiloh.

"I don't know what is happening."

He called me.

"Tell me," he said.

I began to speak of the rage, the self-harming thoughts, the fear, the feelings of powerlessness, and, most of all, the shame.

His voice was soothing. "I will help you. You don't have to do this alone."

A huge wave of relief washed over me; he seemed to understand what was happening to me.

Then Shiloh explained what I had failed to see. This titanic emotional outpouring was the release of the massive amount of emotion that had been suppressed during those years of sexual abuse. That much trauma released all at once made me feel I was being ripped to shreds. The trauma had been a part of me for most of my life. In one sense, I *was* being shredded.

Shiloh spoke with me for a long while, reassuring me that I was through the worst of it. That it would never feel this bad again. The relief I felt at his words was immense. Then he said, "Isn't it beautiful that God provided you with the space to process this? Your work was delayed so that you would have the emotional space to allow this clearing."

He was right. My client had been telling me for weeks that we were "just about to start" on a large project. This kind of delay had never happened to me before. But I ceased resenting how they kept me dangling. Instead of being treated unprofessionally, I was being offered time and space for important inner work.

The next few days unfolded as Shiloh had described. The emotions lessened and then disappeared. A huge space had opened up inside me and I could stand up straight in a way that I had never done before. This translated quite literally to my height, which I discovered a few months later had increased by a quarter of an inch.

A few days later, I awoke in a completely different state.

For the first time in about fifteen years, I was completely shocked to feel intense physical desire.

I had not been in a relationship in fifteen years and all feelings of being interested in or even capable of an intimate relationship were dormant. Further, I had been happy to be in that state. It was so much easier not to feel anything. My two marriages had been deeply traumatic. It was much safer to be alone.

But here was desire, insisting I take notice. I did not wish to. I did not want such dangerous feelings.

Two days passed in this constantly unwelcome state that did not dissipate or lessen or leave me with a moment's peace. Worse, I was desperately ashamed of how out of control I felt.

I was not surprised at all when Shiloh texted me.

"How are you today, Sophia?"

I stared at this message for a long while, unable to respond. I did not wish to speak to him about this. When he had first met me, years prior, I had refused to speak to him about the body dysmorphia that he noted. Far, far less did I wish to discuss this latest development. I did not know what was happening to me and the shame of it left me barely functional.

His next text came after a long while.

"Do you wish to chat?"

I did not. But this was Shiloh, who never judged me.

Shiloh had helped me to see many aspects of myself that I had not understood. A mini-battle raged in me, between shame and a desire for healing.

Another half hour passed before I could respond. I eked out the three letters that I knew would precipitate a call.

"Yes."

He called right away. I told him as succinctly as possible, using the most cryptic words that I could muster, that I was experiencing the worst possible case of what might be called lust, and that it was deeply and profoundly disturbing to me.

He was straightforward.

"So. You have not had a relationship in fifteen years?"

"That's right."

"And this is the first time in fifteen years that you have felt desire?"

"Yes." I swallowed painfully. "But it's not like anything I ever felt before. Ever." I wasn't sure how to describe how completely it had taken me over.

"Right, then," his voice was reassuring in its matter-of-factness, as though I had been speaking of a headache.

"It makes perfect sense. You have had a massive clearing of trauma. Truly massive. It's as if there was a pipe that was clogged. And it was clogged for so long that an enormous amount of water built up beyond that. Now that backed-up water is rushing through the pipe. At some point, it will settle."

His reasonable words did not assuage my near-total hysteria. I nearly shouted. "I can't walk around like this! Does everyone walk around like this? I can't take it! This is disgusting!"

"If you judge yourself, I cannot work with you." He was completely serious. This was his limit.

I gulped. "Okay."

"It is not a negative thing. It is not a positive thing. It simply is what is happening. All will settle, but only if you accept the process."

He spoke to me for a long time of self-acceptance. Of the ways that trauma affects us. Of the process of dealing with trauma of all kinds. As he spoke, it dawned on me that he was not speaking from a textbook. All that he said applied directly to me, even in terms of things that I had never told him. He knew them without me saying them. This was no clinical healing but a spiritual one. I knew the difference. I had seen two different psychotherapists and had told each of my emotional and sexual abuse. Even after years of therapy, I carried the trauma.

"You get to have a full life, Sophia. With relationships and all they have to offer. Now comes the good part. You have worked hard to get to this point and you get to pick the fruit from the tree you have watered. God wants no less for you than this. A full life."

Once again, he had brought me from the brink of

self-loathing to a place of self-acceptance and self-love. His complete lack of judgment of me, of total faith in the process that God had arranged, allowed me to accept myself. There was nothing wrong. Everything was proceeding perfectly on my healing journey.

In retrospect, I realized that when he texted me that August morning a week prior, casually mentioning trauma clearing, that God had used Shiloh to trigger this entire healing. Shiloh had often told me that God tells him to say things and do things, and often he is not told why. I could see, now, how useful Shiloh was to God. Because he never questioned why. He just obeyed.

I put the phone down, a smile on my face. God had things under control. I trusted that it would continue to be this way. Forever. The Divine, eternally caring for me in the most meticulous and perfect of ways.

A few weeks later I had a dream in which I was lying in bed, asleep. In the dream, I awoke to find that all I could see was white. Someone had placed a sheet over my head and I was having trouble breathing. I struggled in panic.

Suddenly, I realized I did not need to be afraid. Total calmness descended and quite deliberately with a power

I had never felt before, I hit upwards forcefully with both arms, repelling my attacker. I pulled the sheet from my head to find that no one was there. With great composure, I strode to the next room to tell my mother, calmly, what had happened. As she began to cry, I comforted her, saying, "It's okay. I'm fine. It will never happen again."

When I awoke, I marveled at the feeling of how iron-like my arms had felt. I had never felt such certitude in my power. But more than the ability to enforce boundaries was the sense of absolute dignity I felt. The childhood experiences of molestation left me with a feeling of vulnerability and shame, preventing me from telling a soul what was happening. With healing, I grasped fully that I had done nothing wrong. My continued feelings of shame and powerlessness were an echo, nothing more. And that echo was banished.

CHAPTER
TWENTY-SEVEN

One day my daughter asked, "Is Shiloh your friend?" The question caught me off guard, mostly because I didn't know the answer. It had never occurred to me to wonder.

"Are we friends?" I asked him.

"Well, what is a friend, Sophia?"

The question stumped me. I have had many people in my life who I called friends. Most were gone. They had either not wished to maintain contact with the new person that I had become or I had drifted away from them when I discovered that my new self would not tolerate the sort of friendship they offered. Or they had just naturally vanished because my lifestyle was an itinerant one.

"I guess fundamentally, it is someone who notices and cares whether or not I am alive," I finally answered.

"Well then, I guess, by that measure, we are friends. Because I care whether or not you are on Earth. But I never label myself. Ever. I am whatever God wishes me to be in each moment."

On any occasion when I happened to be with Shiloh, either walking, in a cafe for tea, or in a restaurant, I noticed that people stared at him. I am sure that I stared at him as well, particularly when I first met him.

Our attention is drawn, I think, by the combination of peace and confidence that he carries. We stare, trying to understand how confidence can look so different in him than in others, not understanding that confidence in God confers a deep peace. What we are seeing, and do not recognize because of its rarity, is true faith.

Shiloh told me once that if someone offered him a wheelbarrow full of gold he would not trade it for even an ounce of knowing God. Over and over again, as we discussed many things both personal and in the world, I found that his deference to God's will surpassed everything. When he spoke of his own life, I could see his patience in waiting for God to realign situations or to guide him in what to do. It was quite beyond anything I imagined possible.

His faith rendered him wholly accepting of everything, so much so that he was nonreactive to even very shocking occurrences. Once he was the recipient of a physical attack and when I saw the wound on his leg, I asked him what he had done when it happened. He said that he just walked away without speaking. But then he went back and left some food on the doorstep of the person who had attacked him, saying he knew they were in a difficult situation.

Once, when we were having tea in a cafe, I became quite emotional because he mentioned one way that I was being self-defeating. I knew he was right but when he pointed it out, it shocked me because I had been completely unaware of it. Despite my emotional state, a part of me was amazed at his presence. I have never seen anyone regard me with that level of acceptance and understanding—his eyes glowed with compassion. I will never forget it because even while my insides were quivering in the effort to avoid crying, a part of me could see that he deeply understood my emotional response to the moment as well as the healing that it represented.

Recently I came across a list of words purported to have no direct translation into English. As I read the list, I stopped short when I came to the Hebrew word *firgun*. It means to be generous and unselfish, to bestow without jealousy or envy. However, it has come to mean so much more than that. *Firgun* means to support someone with love and warmth, expecting nothing in return. Some might call it unconditional love because it means to revel in the joy and good fortune of others.

I instantly thought of Shiloh. He gave freely to me by way of supportive words, time, kindness, and warmth. He expected nothing in return. He never made me feel that I had anything to be ashamed of even though I was often confused, self-defeating, and prideful. He accepted with compassion every single part of me, especially those parts that I didn't wish to acknowledge.

The Finnish have a word that also describes Shiloh perfectly. *Sisu*. It means grit, determination, and tenacity in the face of great odds. In our lives of relative comfort, mental and physical toughness is not something we are often called upon to express. But Shiloh faced extreme physical challenges as well as emotional challenges as a sensitive person in a world that does not value sensitivity. His journey to faith, to God, is a remarkable one filled with great pain and greater miracles. I hope he tells his story one day so that others can also know his remarkably relentless determination.

I was reminded of this unusual combination of *firgun* and *sisu* one day, when I awoke from a strangely vivid dream. In the dream, Shiloh was seated on a low rectangular stone with his back to me. Oddly, my point of view was from behind him, almost as though I were a camera. From the perspective of this dream camera, I could see myself sitting near him closely watching him doing something with an object in his hands. Although from the vantage point of the dream camera I could not see what was in his hands, my sense was that he was sewing something.

Suddenly, the camera zoomed in and I could see that what he held was not an object at all, but flowing colors of energy. There were two distinct energies one orange, yellow and red swirls and the other darker and more well-defined though not any shape I recognized. He was fitting these two forms together, meticulously and intricately.

I asked "What is that?" and instantly the answer arose: the energies of the masculine and the feminine.

When I woke up. The dream was so vivid that I left Shiloh a voice message relating what I had seen.

"That is fascinating," he texted back. "It sounds like a bridging of energies into divine wholeness."

A man of God would indeed combine the attributes of strength and compassion, I thought, and the meaning of the dream clicked into place.

Over the years, Shiloh told me many things about God and the truth of this world that I have not written here. These things are not mine to tell and I could not do them justice even if I tried.

Once I asked him a benign sort of question and his answer was astonishingly far beyond what I imagined could be stimulated by a tiny question. I wondered how he could know these things, universal truths of the nature of all things, and I asked him where he had learned it all.

"I didn't learn it," he said. "Everything comes from God." He told me that he never read books, even as a child, saying that he did not clutter his mind with others' words when God tells him all that he needed to know.

CHAPTER
TWENTY-EIGHT

The small stones on the beach near the marina crunched under me as I settled near the water's edge. I was preparing to spend the summer in the States and to attend a family wedding.

Shiloh had warned me that going home could be challenging. He said that when I am around people who have known me for a long time, they may set me back.

I was surprised. I felt sure I could maintain the state of trust in God I had worked so hard to reach. But that is not what Shiloh meant. He said that I had changed how I felt about myself, the way I interacted with God, and the way I saw the world. But others had not changed how they thought of me. They still saw me as the person I was years and years ago. He warned me that the collective weight of their ideas about me could affect me deeply.

It made sense why Shiloh always asked me to not judge others. My thoughts affected others just as theirs affected me.

"This is one reason that it has been so helpful to leave home, to travel, and move around frequently," he said. "People do not have a chance to form judgments of you."

Suddenly, I was sure this phenomenon was why God had isolated me. The absence of prolonged contact with others spared me their ideas and judgments. I was free to grow and change as guided by God. I had been upset by my isolation, but it was a necessary step on a path of change and growth.

I waded into the water and breathed a heartfelt thanks to God for all that had happened to me. It had been a long time in coming, this peace that I had longed for, and knowing God as my eternal friend and guide. I said a silent a prayer of acknowledgment into the water. *Thank You for always being there for me, even when I don't feel You, see You, or hear You. I know You always care for me perfectly.*

I meant it deeply and tears welled at the feeling of God's love for me and for this world.

I returned to my towel close to the water's edge and settled once again looking down on the sea at my feet.

Within a minute or so, on the surface of the water, a

chaotic rippling formed in the shape of two, large conjoined circles. Within seconds the source of the rippling became obvious. Tiny fish began leaping from the water, high into the air, their bodies flashing in the sunlight. It looked for all the world like a fountain, with sparkling fish instead of water droplets. I had never seen anything like it.

I knew instantly that God sent His fish, directly in front of me in a large infinity sign at least ten feet across, to show me His joy that I recognized His hand in my life and to reaffirm His promise to care for me, which extended into infinity.

On the beach behind me, I heard exclamations.

"Look! Look!" Several people ran forward to get closer to the incredible sight. The little leaping fish were so close to the shore that some began to land on the rocks and flop around. Some people knelt to scoop up the tiny fish that had propelled themselves onto the beach, tossing them back into the water.

When the fountain stopped, I sat for a while enjoying the lovely moment. After those rescuing the tiny fish went back to their towels, a man behind me began throwing rocks over my head onto the shore in front of me, shattering the sacredness of the moment. I picked up my towel and walked back to the boat, feeling quite content.

Along the way, I spied a man who looked very much like my first husband. An unkind thought crossed my mind.

Seconds later, I felt a pronounced *thunk* on my forehead between my eyes, as though something had dropped from the sky. I stopped short, wondering what had happened. I was in the open air and no one was around. I looked down and around at my feet to see whether there was a large beetle or other large insect. I saw nothing, but the message became instantly clear. My unkind thought was unacceptable.

I told Shiloh about the fish fountain. It was nice to share the beautiful moment at the sea with him and he shared in the joy that was God bestowing a sign of His presence. When I told him of the subsequent thump on my forehead, he agreed that it was a perfect correction.

"It is always helpful when we have quick responses to our actions. We have to be careful with our thoughts, don't we?"

After the busy and eventful family wedding in Texas, I stayed blissfully alone for two weeks in a house in a quiet neighborhood where I could do a bit of work in peace and recover from the intense pace of the festivities.

Early one day, I received a voice message from Shiloh inquiring as to how the wedding had gone. At the end of his message, he shared an interesting story of the remarkable way that he had received a monetary gift from God. My heart swelled in joy for him, and I recall thinking how much God must love Shiloh to provide for him so surely.

That's when I heard God say: "It can be this way for you, too."

Along with the words flowed a wave of extreme clarity. Instantly, I grasped my mistake. I was separating myself from God in a fundamental way. I thought that God took care of Shiloh perfectly because he was chosen. But the truth is that Shiloh receives all that he needs because he is perfectly surrendered and aligned with God's will. If I were aligned with God's will, then it would be the same for me. Every step along the path of my soul's journey would be divinely supported. It was truly a mind-blowing moment to know that God cared for me as much as He cared for Shiloh.

It seems almost incredible that I didn't know I was creating a wall between myself and God. After God's declaration that Shiloh was chosen, I placed him on a pedestal. I thought of Shiloh as special and myself as one of the multitudinous not-special people. It is certainly true that Shiloh has a specific life mission, chosen by God, because of the attributes of his soul. But I must never forget that I have a soul path as well, and I am supported on that path by God. As does everyone.

At that moment, I understood that there was no free pass for me. I didn't get to relax, thinking that Shiloh has to do the hard work of aligning with God while I watch and marvel. Like Shiloh, and everyone else interested in knowing God, I must assiduously cultivate my connection to God.

I tingled with the implications of this understanding. Divine support is not randomly meted out in certain moments to certain people. It flows constantly, and it is up to us to align with God in full faith and surrender.

The next morning, I sat on the front porch in the calmness of the early morning, resting in a feeling of great contentment. A memory dropped like a pebble into the still pool of my mind. Shiloh had tried to tell me what God had whispered in my ear the day before. Many, many times.

"Anyone can follow this path. Anyone can surrender to God if they truly wish it," he had said.

I thought I had known what he meant. That I should consult God on all decisions. But that is a superficial understanding.

To truly surrender to God meant to give up myself. It was not enough to agree to do what God says, but instead to have no ideas. No thoughts of who I was and what I thought of God. Only then could I fully know God. This is what Shiloh had told me over and over in various ways over the years. Finally, it had clicked deeply.

I wanted to acknowledge to Shiloh that I understood what he had been trying to say for so long. I wanted him to know that I understood that my life had been perfectly orchestrated for my path, exactly as he had always told me. The pain, betrayal, confusion, and self-doubt set the perfect stage for me to turn consistently to He who would never betray me. God.

All of this, I summed in three words.

"God is great."

"The greatest thing in this life is knowing how great God is," he responded.

The next day as I worked in the quiet of the morning, it dawned on me that my three months in Texas were nearly over. Soon I would need to leave and I had nowhere to go. Without a moment of concern or worry, I asked God to take care of my next movements and then I returned to my work. I was sure something would show itself, and I didn't concern myself in the least with finding it.

Within a few hours, I received a text message. An invitation to stay at a beach house on Cape Cod, courtesy of a friend. It was a delightful offer, and I accepted readily, thanking God for orchestrating the situation into existence.

Once at the beautiful cottage, every morning I walked to the beach to swim in the cool water before the crowds arrived for the day. Early one morning I was treading water, when I felt a shiver of fear slice through me. The book that God asked me to write about Shiloh was not going well. I hadn't written anything useful in at least six months. I felt quite unable to continue. Maybe it won't be good enough, I thought. Even if I do finish it, maybe what I write won't accomplish what God wished, whatever that was. It deeply frightened me that I would not be able to do what God asked.

I tried to dispel the fear by telling myself that God knew my limitations and would not have asked me to do something impossible. But I was acutely aware of my inadequacies, particularly in comparison to Shiloh. He had such a clear understanding of God's ways and I was such a novice on the path, prone to falling in holes and lacking insight into myself and others. However, the first thing Shiloh taught me was to reject any self-judgment, and the second to give all my burdens to God. So, I gave this one as well. *I know I am limited. Please God show me the way.*

I waded out of the water. Shrugging on my sweatshirt against the morning chill, I turned to leave. As I did so, I looked up and gasped. Through the abundant grey clouds, sunlight streamed in a beautiful burst of light.

As I gazed at the lovely sight, I heard Spirit whisper in my ear, "Even through the clouds, the sun makes a beautiful pattern."

I knew, then, it would be well. Whatever I wrote, however inarticulate and unclear, it would be enough. I would not fail God.

CHAPTER
TWENTY-NINE

After spending the summer in the States, I returned to Sirius to prepare her for winter. I scraped and sanded and varnished the exterior wood with gusto, for I had only a short time before I needed to leave.

I was heading to an island in the Baltic Sea. I had been enticed by the prospect of remote accommodation and proximity to nature, which would hopefully lend inspiration to write.

When I arrived, I saw that the owner of the island lived in the main house on top of a hill while I stayed in a cabin at the water's edge. Although the forested area was quite beautiful and there was abundant wildlife, the situation didn't turn out to be supportive for either contemplation or writing. The living conditions were fairly inhospitable and the cabin had no running water.

When winter set in early, I was quite cold. The cabin was not well-insulated and equipped only with a tiny radiator and a single blanket for the bed. The temperature dropped below freezing each night. One evening, I huddled under the covers with my gloves and hat on, long before I would normally have gone to bed. I was miserable and ashamed that I was not handling it well. The emotional reaction to the situation was causing me more pain than the cold. I said as much to Shiloh.

"I will pray for you," he texted.

I prayed fervently for acceptance, knowing that surrender would bring me peace.

The next morning when I went up to the main house, the owner let me in the door and offered me a cup of tea, as usual. She was training me to test blood sugar levels of her diabetic cat so I could take care of him when she went on vacation. He was a beautiful, old Norwegian forest cat, and as I scratched him beneath the chin, she said, "Are you warm enough in the cabin?"

My head snapped upward. I had been in the cabin for several weeks and she had not asked me this.

"No," I said, waiting to see what God had wrought.

"Well, let me give you my big radiator." She pointed to

a massive portable radiator that stood in the corner. "I can order a new one."

"Thank you," I said, not sure why I was stunned that God had acted so quickly in response to Shiloh's prayers.

Soon enough, though, I began to chafe under the other challenging conditions, particularly under the assumption that I was happy to provide labor on command. I could see that my initial willingness to help with outdoor tasks such as splitting wood had opened the door to expectation. One day, the owner asked me to move the rowboat so it would be readily available for her in the morning. The high winds and rain were quite the deterrent. I declined, knowing she had a different route open to her, one that didn't require that particular boat. But she insisted it was necessary and that I, as the stronger of the two of us, should do it. I made the journey despite my better judgment, and I struggled to keep the boat on course. The final docking was difficult. Each time I shipped the oars to get near the pontoon, the wind blew the boat into the reeds and I had to start over. This was my fault, and I knew it.

Once again, Shiloh helped me see that God was offering me an opportunity to treat myself with care and decline to get involved in issues that had nothing to do with me.

Then he said something that surprised me. "I see inside you a dark line from your mind all down through your body. It is an idea that was placed in your mind when you were very young and spreads through you. 'I'm not good enough,' that dark line says. Do you see how this makes it difficult for you to receive what God wishes for you? It affects everything, because it is deep inside you, so deep that you might not see it."

But I did see it, though only in its reflection. I saw it in how I always tried to be a good person, out of fear that I was not. I saw it because I always tried to be perfect in all that I did, desperately hoping to overcome my feeling of inadequacy. I saw it because I always tried to make people like me by being helpful, volunteering for all kinds of things.

"How can I get rid of this?" I whispered.

"Pray. God knows exactly how to heal all things and will bring to you all that you need to heal, if you ask." Then he advised me to recognize when others do not respect me. He spoke for quite a while explaining how to do this. He told me how deeply my life would change if I could fully accept that God had given me a great gift, this life, and that I didn't need to do anything to earn it. He said that if I could integrate this fully, that I would see everyone around me treating me differently. "You might find this person on the island with you will start to treat you as a guest rather than a laborer."

Then he reminded me, because he knew my tendencies

quite well, that this change was not an activity or an action. It was not something I needed to *do*. Rather, it was an internal shift to make in how I viewed myself.

That night I prayed for self-love and self-respect and the removal of the dark line of self-doubt. I prayed to recognize the moments in which I was not valuing myself and the gift of life God had given me.

Soon enough I had my opportunity. The owner knocked on the door of the cabin as I was writing one day. She handed me some of the final windfall apples of the season that she had gathered from beneath her neighbor's tree.

"Thank you," I said, grateful for the kindness.

"Oh, by the way, in a few days, I will have the electric bill from the last two months for us to split."

I nodded. She was reminding me that before I had arrived she had asked me to pay for electricity in the cabin. The prior year the gas shortage in this area of Europe caused electricity rates to be ten times more costly than normal and she had been worried about the extra cost of heating a summer cabin.

When I agreed to pay for the electricity, I had not known the cabin was without running water. I had not known that I would be asked to urinate in the bushes or a host of other issues that made my life quite challenging.

I looked at the circumstances, careful to only see the

situation without judging her or myself. I decided that this was not a reasonable request. I was in a marginally livable situation with duties that had been unknown to me when I agreed to the situation. Further, the electricity rates were not elevated this year as they had been in the past. Therefore, I owed her nothing.

When she approached me again, such was my feeling of correct action that there was zero emotion behind it.

"I think that given the circumstances and given heating costs are not what they were last year, you should reconsider asking me to pay for electricity," I said, neutrally. I was just stating a fact.

She accepted my assertion. I was pleased at how simple it was to say what I thought and to say it in a way that did not blame.

The circumstances on the island continued to be difficult, though. The electricity went out because of a surge and then the internet failed. A pipe in the bathhouse burst and the water had to be shut off for several days.

My feet were dry, cracked, and bleeding. They hurt even when I wasn't standing, and I became concerned they may be infected. At this point, I was ready to leave despite having originally agreed to stay until mid-December. But the owner wanted to leave for another vacation, and she wanted me to care for her cat while she was gone.

As soon as I mentioned leaving, she changed entirely. She began to ask me what I needed. More heat? Got it. Laundry? Done. Dishes washed and delivered to my doorstep? Yes.

Shiloh had predicted this change, and it was a welcome one. Once the water was restored in the bathhouse, I decided to stay.

While the owner was away, with her permission, I spent time in the main house with its warm fireplace and I cooked in the large kitchen with the luxury of running water at my fingertips. It was a welcome change from the hot plate in my cabin.

One evening in December, I was back in the little cabin for the night when I saw a text from Shiloh.

I called him. He did not sound himself.

"Shiloh, is everything okay?"

"Oh, it is just a challenging time, Sophia."

This was not a man who complained. Ever. If he said things were challenging, they were truly unbearable. I asked if he wished to speak about it.

With barely any emphasis, as though it were a quite disinteresting topic, he told me of an accumulation of ill treatment, ending with some shocking specifics of things that had been done to him and to his van. Before he could take a breath to speak again, something quite bizarre happened.

The room tilted slightly and I heard the screeching sound that boards make when they are straining tightly against their nails. The entire cabin shook for a few seconds and the windows rattled in their frames. I recognized the disorienting feeling; the earth had moved.

"Wait! Wait…something is happening." I threw the phone on the bed and ran outside. Of course, there was nothing, but the night and the snow.

"Shiloh, I could swear there was an earthquake," I said when I returned after a quick check. It was nearly 10:00 PM and although there might be blasting in the area, certainly no one was blasting in the dark on a Friday night.

I knew it was a message. If God's messenger was being ill-treated then why wouldn't the earth shake in protest?

The next morning the deck outside creaked when I stepped on it. It had never been anything but solid before. I dropped to my knees and saw the nails had popped slightly. I could not imagine anything other than the movement of the building itself or the earth underneath it that could cause nails to pop like that.

I continued to work on the children's book series, the one that had begun while I was living on Sirius two years prior. I was working on the second book while I searched for an illustrator for the first one.

"You can create the art for the book, Sophia." Shiloh seemed confident.

I was no artist. I found it difficult to draw anything but straight lines. I tried to explain. "Shiloh, I have tried my whole life to draw. I am unbelievably bad at it, despite many attempts. Many."

"I think you can do it," he said.

Years earlier, I had uncovered a long-forgotten memory of being ridiculed, quite cruelly, for a picture I had drawn when I was very young. It was why I felt blocked at every turn when I tried to draw even the simplest images.

"Everyone has the ability to create art," Shiloh said. "It is only a belief that you cannot that makes it difficult."

I said nothing. I had tried, and failed spectacularly, many times. Even remembering the long-ago trauma had not helped me to release the block. I had eventually accepted that I would never be able to draw.

It was difficult for me, the time I spent on the island, and Shiloh knew how much I struggled. A few days later, I spoke with him again. As usual, the conversation uplifted me. The truth of God's ways was a message I never tired of hearing.

I hung up the phone and, suddenly, I wanted to draw. But

I didn't feel to try. I felt that I *could* draw. After viewing the video of an artist drawing a very realistic pair of lips with nothing but a pencil, I tried it. I had never drawn anything that was even remotely similar to the original. But I was stunned beyond belief—this pair of beautiful, realistic lips I had drawn nearly leaped off the page in three dimensions. I took a picture of the lips and sent them to Shiloh.

"I guess you were right," I said.

He called me.

"Well done!" he said. "Those are quite realistic."

"It was so strange, Shiloh. After we hung up, I was just kind of in that joyful state, you know?" He knew what I meant.

"I didn't even think about it. I didn't say 'Hey, I want to try.' I just knew that I could."

"You know, Sophia, I saw that you could draw, a few days ago. I simply knew you could. And then you could."

Goosebumps rose on my arms.

"I have to be careful what I focus on," he said.

He had focused on an abscess in my tooth a year prior and it had disappeared. Now the blockage to being able to draw had disappeared.

To suddenly be able to draw, and so late in my life, felt nothing short of miraculous.

CHAPTER
THIRTY

One day, after completing the morning cat duties, watering the many indoor plants, and doing a bit of work for a client, I decided to take a shower for the sole purpose of softening my sore feet and applying balm to the cracks. I went to the deliciously warm bathhouse just after midday. The sun only shone six hours per day this time of year and it was glancing through the curtains, already well on its way to sundown. When I reached out to move the shower curtain aside, I gasped. My bare right arm was covered in sunlit flowers.

The sun was streaming through the lacy, flowered curtains. And when I looked, I could see the reflection of my body in the glass of the shower. I was covered in golden flowers. The effect was so delightful that I grabbed my phone and took several pictures. For the first time in my life, I did not feel ashamed of my body. The moment was so magical that I didn't want it to end. The winter sun shone golden on my skin and I was suffused with a glow of love for this body, this gift from God, that was covered in flowers. Eventually, I stepped, smiling with delight, into the shower. After four minutes, which was the full length of the hot water available to me, I stepped out onto the tiled floor. The magic was gone. The sun, already low in the sky, had dipped below the tree line and no longer shone through the windows.

But it had been enough. I happily dried myself and dressed. I walked slowly to the cabin in the snow, enjoying the revelation that, at last, I was able to love my body.

When Shiloh first met me, he said, quite accurately, that I had a problem with body image. From that moment onward, he had not mentioned my body. He had never reassured me; he had never commented on my size or shape or anything superficial about me. Yet, here I was, nearly six years later, accepting and celebrating my body, which was, if anything, older and worse for wear.

Shiloh had gone straight to the root of all my problems. A lack of self-love. He showed me that through trusting God, I could accept myself for who I was—a child of God, beloved by God, endlessly supported by the Creator who gave me life. The body dysmorphia was simply a symptom of self-loathing and fear that I was not good enough.

I sat on my bed and considered the ways my life had changed since meeting Shiloh. My feet no longer hurt; my libido that had been long dead was restored; my body dysmorphia was gone; lactose intolerance of long duration had inexplicably disappeared; and the psoriasis in my eyebrows that had come and gone for 10 years was gone. What's more, I could draw; I had written a book for children, I had begun to play the violin and to take ballet lessons, all of which had been lifelong dreams. The biggest change though, was that Shiloh had brought me to God. I felt truly grateful for all that God had given me and for Shiloh's guidance and healing.

The next day I received a text from Shiloh.

"I have a message to deliver to you. From God. Can I please deliver this to you without you reading too much into it?"

"Okay," I said. Not knowing how completely I would fail his simple request.

"I was praying last night and God said 'Ask Sophia how often she examines her breasts for lumps'."

In that instant, my life turned upside down.

"I never do," I managed, shaking, after the initial shock of his message subsided.

"Well, you might consider it. Monitoring our bodies is our duty."

I gulped air, my body rigid with shock.

How could this be happening? All that I had been through was not enough? I was beside myself with incredulity.

I knew Shiloh felt my extreme upset.

"Thank you for the message," I texted.

Then, I completely lost my sanity.

"What are You doing to me?" I screamed at God. I pounded the wall of the cabin. It was quite firm and it hurt my hand. God did not answer. But if God had told Shiloh I needed to check for a lump, it must be for the worst reason.

I burst into tears, shaken by the ultimate irony. One day I was celebrating my body for the first time and the next day, it was a ticking bomb.

Sleep was impossible. I vacillated between shock and devastation all night. The next day when I picked up my phone, I saw that Shiloh had messaged.

"Remember that because God asked you this does not mean anything is wrong. You have no idea what it means."

I was not heartened by his words. I could not imagine a single scenario in which God would have prompted Shiloh to ask me such a question unless to warn me of something seriously wrong. In the mirror I saw a large, pulsing vein snaking across my forehead. The thumping in my head unnerved me as much as the thought of a cancer in my breast. I cried out of sheer powerlessness. I had no immediate access to health care and there was nothing I could do, not for days.

I went into the sauna in the bathhouse and lit the fire. I huddled, distraught and shaking, as the wood stove heated the small, dark room. After several hours, all that Shiloh had told me of surrender and acceptance and trust finally kicked in. I had been telling God that I pledged my life to Him but when it came right down to it, I had not. I knew what I had to do.

My life was not my own, so I could not be angry if it was taken. This life was God's gift and whether or not I lost a breast or lost my life, it was not for me to say.

In the sauna, with the sweat trickling down my back and standing in beads on my face, I formally accepted the possibility of cancer. *As You will. As You will. Whatever happens next, I leave entirely up to you. Whatever you give me, I accept. You know best, and I do not. I accept this, whatever it is.*

I repeated this over and over, and I descended into a deep state of peace.

Finally, I did a breast self-exam.

When I found the lump, it was unmistakable. Near the

armpit on the right portion of the breast. In the area where lumps are most likely to be cancerous.

I felt completely calm.

I had prepared myself to accept anything and now that I had found the lump, it was just a thing to deal with. Like a flat tire. Or a broken phone.

I waited until the next morning to let him know. "Shiloh, I found a lump."

"What will you do?"

"I will see to getting a mammogram. I don't know after that."

I was one week away from leaving the island. I tried to find a place in town to get a mammogram but it did not work out. The area was too remote, and I had no car. Plus, I had the cat to care for.

I had already booked a flight to Batumi, in Georgia, where I had stayed years earlier. It was much warmer than Sweden and it was inexpensive. I felt sure I could get a mammogram there.

CHAPTER
THIRTY-ONE

On Christmas Eve I stared out the window of my hotel room in Batumi. I had spent a week settling in and trying to find a place to live but had found nothing. I was equally unsuccessful in scheduling a mammogram. Inexplicably so. Even a trip to the hospital had yielded nothing but frustration. It was, I knew, time to quit pushing and allow God to handle things.

Two days of rain had prevented me from enjoying the sea and the surrounding area. The feeling of being trapped was quite acute. I was not sure whether I should go or stay; I had no idea what God wished me to do. But in three days, I needed to check out of the hotel and either leave the country or find a more permanent place to stay. I had no plan.

Shiloh texted, as he always does when I am feeling quite lost.

"How are you today, Sophia?"

"Trying not to stare too hard into the fog," I replied, referring to the mystery that Shiloh had said was God working in our lives.

His reply, in which he referred to the fog as a gift conferring peace and simplicity, was poetic. But I was not moved to a place of peace by his words. Instead, I bluntly described the desperation of my situation.

"Shiloh, I have no idea where I am to go in three days when I must check out of this hotel."

"All will align. Trust."

Until now, trust had been well within reach. After all, I had money and health. But now I was faced with an entirely different situation. I found trust to be vastly more difficult to achieve when my life was in the balance. I wasn't sure whether or not there was a cancer in my breast. I did not know whether I could afford treatment if there was. I did not know where I should go for such treatment if needed.

Years before, Shiloh had told me that I was hanging onto a spiritual ledge, tightly with both hands. "Take the leap of faith," he had urged. "God is there for you."

I sat on the edge of the bed staring out at the night, at the darkest spot where I knew lay the Black Sea. It was nearly

9 PM on Christmas Eve. God was calling me. It was time to take that leap.

"Okay, God. It is just You and me." I spoke as though a friend were in the room, one who didn't mind seeing my red, unhappy face or my dripping nose. I imagined the basket that Shiloh had told me about. The basket in which I should place all my worries and pain before handing it to God. I began to fill it.

"God, I'm so alone." It was Christmas and there was not a single soul to celebrate with. I put loneliness in the basket.

I had just come off a year in which I had stayed in twelve different places and this was the thirteenth. I was emotionally, mentally, and physically tired. The trip here with its 16-hour layover in Istanbul had been brutal and I had sworn that I would stay put in Batumi and rest. But that was not to be. I needed medical care, and I was having no luck finding it here.

"God, I don't know where to go. I am so tired of this way of life, where I have no home base and I have to travel all the time." I placed those dark feelings in the basket, too.

"God, I am so lost as to how to deal with getting the mammogram and the idea that there might be something truly wrong that I have to deal with, without insurance, without help. It just feels too much." I put those worries in the basket.

"God, if you wish my life to be over on this planet and for

me to return to You, then I release that to You as well. My life is Yours." I put my life in the basket.

It was the scariest thing I'd ever done.

I visualized a large red Christmas bow on that basket, and I handed it to God.

I sat on the bed, staring out into the dark, breathing. There was nothing more to do. I could not think about tomorrow. I could not think about next week or a few months from now. I had no idea what was going to happen. But I could rest at this moment.

"Right now, all is well. In this moment, all is well." I repeated it, for several minutes, mantra-like. It was true. I had a place to stay for the night. I was warm. I had food and water. What else did I need?

Suddenly, there was a knock at the door.

I didn't know anyone in this country. I had no idea who would knock on my door late at night in a gated building.

When I opened the door, I saw three young men wearing Santa Claus outfits. They said something in Russian, of course, and seeing my confusion, one of the men immediately smiled and switched to perfect English. He asked me where I was from and when I told him, all three exclaimed because Georgia is not such a common destination for Americans.

"We are collecting money on behalf of a school for children. They have made these ornaments and we wonder if you would like to donate? The ornament is 15 lari, but you can donate whatever you like."

I excused myself, smiling at the remarkable timing, and found my purse. I handed a twenty-lari bill to the man holding the angel ornaments. He spread the wooden shapes like a deck of cards, and I selected one with a star in the lower part of the gown.

"Thank you," he said. "Merry Christmas and welcome to our country."

I closed the door and hugged that ornament to me, laughing with delight. Then, I placed it on the table, took a picture, and sent it to Shiloh.

"Look what showed up at my door."

"It is a beautiful angel," Shiloh said after I explained where I had received the only reminder of Christmas in my sterile hotel room. "God is saying 'No matter where you are, or what is happening, I can get an angel to you. Just trust in Me.'"

"It is very nice to have a human reminder of that."

"God can reach us anywhere."

I put the phone down, heartened at the small gesture that meant that God had received my basket of woes and had sent me a little Christmas gift to comfort me.

The next morning, I awoke with a sense of peace and calmness that befitted Christmas Day. Into my mind dropped the next chapter of the second children's book I was writing. I leaped from the bed. It had been weeks since I had received the inspiration to write. The chapter flowed easily onto the page and when I was finished, I decided to treat myself to a nice lunch.

It was raining softly, unlike the torrential cold rains of the prior two days. I walked the boulevard along the seafront, enjoying the smell of the pine trees. When I found the vegan restaurant I was looking for, I stepped in the door. A woman looked toward me and said something in Russian.

"I'm sorry I don't speak Russian."

After a few halting words in English, she turned to two patrons who were just standing up and putting on their coats. She spoke rapid-fire Russian, and I waited patiently.

One of the couple turned to me. "The owner says to tell you that she is closed. Today is the day that she makes the desserts for the rest of the week." She indicated her male companion, continuing, "We are here because she forgot to lock the door, and when we came in, she decided to feed us anyway. She says you can eat too but there are only three things available for you to choose from."

I turned to the owner. I knew she would understand me. "It's okay if you're closed. I can come back tomorrow."

She smiled, "No, no. Sit down. You can eat."

I smiled gratefully. The angel, the book chapter inspiration, and now a meal at one of the few vegan restaurants in the area. What a lovely Christmas.

When she brought me the tofu scramble with micro greens and avocado, I nearly cried. It had been a long time since I had seen such fresh and lovely vegan food. When I was nearly finished, she brought a basket full of citrus fruit to me, asking me to choose one. I selected a clementine, and thought, again, of how lucky I was. A sweet treat on Christmas day.

I finished my tea and rose to go to the back counter to pay. The owner came toward me holding the card payment device. But when she looked up at me, I saw her face change and she said, "This is a gift for you."

"What?" I asked, confused.

"Today is a gift for you," she said. "My thanks. For coming here when it is so cold and rainy." Her smile was genuine. I don't think she knew it was Christmas for me. But I felt the gifts to me had multiplied. Not only had she opened her door on a day when she did not have to, she had given me free food. Delicious, healthy vegan food.

"Thank you. That is such a beautiful thing," I said, and I meant it.

It was the nicest Christmas I had spent in a long time. I deeply felt the message from God. *See how I take care of you when you let Me?*

The next day I received an email from a man in England who was renting a spare room on a weekly basis. I had emailed him the week before when I was desperately trying to figure the best place to get a mammogram. I had not heard from him and figured it was no longer available.

"Are you still interested? I can show you the place this week."

I wrote back that I could be there on Friday afternoon. I did not tell him I was in a different country. Quickly I searched for flights. I saw three days of low airfare bounded by extremely high airfares—a window of opportunity for me to fly to the UK without breaking the bank. I took it.

CHAPTER
THIRTY-TWO

I sat on the edge of the exam table. The doctor and the nurse stood side by side facing me as I held a sheet over my chest.

"We are going to examine your breasts," the doctor said. At his words, I dropped the sheet. He and the nurse froze.

"I was supposed to do that, right?"

The nurse rushed to reassure me. "That's exactly what we needed."

But I knew I had bared my breasts before they expected it. I, who had been so ashamed of my body, surprised both myself and others by not feeling at all shy.

The doctor performed a visual examination and then said, "Where do you feel the lump?"

I pointed to the spot that I had palpated many times in the past four weeks.

He placed the tips of his fingers on the spot. "Yes, there is something there." He made a little "x" on my skin.

"But even if I hadn't found anything I would refer you for a mammogram because you have not had one in twenty years." He shook his head. "I don't know how that could have happened."

The nurse smiled and joked, "I think that is some kind of record."

They were trying to put me at ease, I knew. But I was calm. I was prepared for whatever happened. I had been prepared for weeks, from that moment in the hotel room in Batumi when I gave my health and my life to God.

I was taken immediately to a room with a large machine and a woman waiting to press my breasts between two plates.

The mammogram showed nothing. However, the breast margins are difficult to see on a mammogram and an ultra-sound quickly ensued. In a matter of moments, the doctor placed the transducer on the mark on my skin.

"Ah, there it is." To spare me any anxiety, he went on immediately. "This is good news. It is a fatty nodule. There is no chance that this is cancer, and it cannot turn into cancer."

I was very calm. "That is wonderful. Thank you so much."

I dressed quickly and went to the receptionist to pay the hefty fees for the visit. The receptionist eyed me warily, so I put her mind at rest. "It was good news."

"Oh, congratulations!" Then, she dropped her voice and tears shone in her eyes as she said, "You have no idea how difficult it is to see these women coming in and out of here. Just last week, a woman was diagnosed in the late stages—she probably won't see another Christmas."

I gave her my credit card. When she handed it back, she said earnestly, "Go and live your best life."

"Thank you. I will."

Over dinner that night, I reflected on my muted response to the good news. I had received job offers that had made me ten times happier.

I was grateful not to go through surgery and deal with all that a cancer diagnosis entails. I was certainly glad to be healthy. But the truth was that I had already given my life to God. Whether or not I lived or died no longer felt like my business. I did not wish for illness and I did not wish for wellness. I simply wished for God's will.

It might seem odd that I did not ask Shiloh to tell me whether the lump was cancerous or that I did not expect him to heal me had it turned out to be something serious. I have no doubt that he could have done both.

But any expectation that I might have for Shiloh to take away pain, to ease physical ailments, or to cure me of any disease would be a violation of an agreement that I had made with God and with Shiloh several years into our mentoring relationship.

Once I understood what Shiloh was offering me—an opportunity to establish a true connection with God—to rely on Shiloh would be an abdication of my duty to do my part in forging that connection. I was not asking for a one-time healing or guidance regarding a single issue but for a deep connection to the Divine. This meant a deep commitment to inner work, work that Shiloh guided me through but that I needed to do myself.

When I had a question, often in response to a challenge, I would say to God, 'If this is something that I can't understand on my own, please ask Shiloh to call me.' At times, I would get a call from Shiloh within one or two minutes of this request. Other times there would be no response and I would know that whatever I faced, I needed to work out without his help.

Further, Shiloh had important work of his own and I could not assume that his energy, time, and focus should be on me. When I hurt my wrist, I did not call him. He sensed something was wrong, and he contacted me. The healing was spontaneously performed in that moment, without my asking for it. When I told him about my tooth abscess, I did not ask for, nor expect, a healing. I trusted that if God wished me to have specific information or a specific healing then Shiloh would offer it.

Shiloh told me many times that the path of faith means allowing life to happen, guided by God and without expectation as to how it should progress. If, along the way, God inspired to Shiloh to spontaneously take away some pain, then I was glad to receive it. But it was not up to me to direct that process.

When I was having trouble scheduling the mammogram in Georgia, Shiloh brought up what he knew I would not ask. Forthright as always, he let me know that God had asked him not to reveal the outcome to me.

"This is an important process for you, and I must let you go through it," he said.

I'm sure it would have been easier for him to simply tell me that it was a benign lump but it would have deprived me of the opportunity of surrendering my life to God.

Even if God had not told me He had chosen Shiloh, I would have known to trust him. If Shiloh were interested in feeling powerful or underscoring his abilities or had any wish to feed the needs of an ego, he could have easily told me what he saw or waved his hand to fix things. Over the six years in which he guided me, I never noted a single instance in which he acted out of a desire to be seen as powerful, to show off his skills, to receive kudos. He used his gifts in service of God, not himself.

A week after the good news, I rested on Sirius in the marina, awaiting some direction as to where to go next. Suddenly, I recalled that while I was on the island in the Baltic, Shiloh had given me another message, one that I had ignored. It came rushing back to me in that quiet moment.

"Sophia, God asked me to say something to you. 'Jonah and the whale.' "

Thoroughly perplexed, I had asked. "What does it mean?"

Shiloh had declined to answer. "That is all I can say."

I have not studied the Bible much but it is a well-known story. Jonah had been tossed overboard by seamen who feared he was the reason that the weather was threatening their ship. He was swallowed by a whale and was inside the belly of the whale for three days. Then he had prayed to God and the whale coughed him up and he was saved. What could Jonah have to do with me?

On the island, I had forgotten all about the Jonah-and-the-whale message in the duress of living in a place that required so much attention to basic needs and the added stress of finding a breast lump.

Now that I recalled this message, I felt chagrined I had not taken it seriously. I searched online and re-read the story, several times. I had no idea what God wished me to know about Jonah. I read various interpretations. Nothing seemed to have any meaning relevant to me. I needed to ask God for help. God could tell me what He meant.

That evening as I prepared for bed, I prayed for understanding. *Dearest God, please tell me. What did You mean by Jonah and the whale? What does this parable have to do with me?*

The next morning, I awoke and in that moment between sleep and wakefulness, the answer filled me, piercing like a lance into my heart.

Like Jonah, I had not done what God asked. I had not finished the book that God had asked me to write about Shiloh.

Despite immediate mental protestations that I was not Jonah, I knew it was true. I was afraid to finish the book. I was afraid to be judged for writing such a book. I was afraid it would not be good enough. I had not been diligent in complying with what God asked me to do. My life had become grinding and painful because of it. I endured many challenges and even agonized over my health because I was not doing what God asked.

Immediately, I felt a renewed determination. I could not ignore God's request any longer. Instantly, the inspiration to write the next chapter in the book arrived in my mind. I leaped from bed and began to write and did not stop for 6 hours. The next day I wrote again. At least 10,000 words flowed in those two days.

I texted Shiloh. "I understand the meaning of Jonah and the whale as it applies to me."

He had allowed me to discover my error. Shiloh had helped clear my blockages, showed me a life of faith, and let me know that when I ask from the heart, I can receive answers from God.

Within a few days of this renewed writing vigor, I discovered a place to stay in Scotland, housesitting in a cottage on the grounds of a castle where there were few residents, abundant trees, a river, and no pets to care for. I could tend a garden, which I sorely missed in my itinerant life. I could use their car. The end date was open, and I could leave early if it became necessary. It was as though every single thing that I wished for, had instantly come true.

I was in the flow of God's Grace once again.

CHAPTER
THIRTY-THREE

I don't know why I was so fortunate to receive the mentoring that Shiloh offered. I am not unusual or particularly deserving. I had a lot of strikes against me: twice-divorced, former Catholic, former agnostic, former pagan, and former new-ager with a deeply troubled past and a long list of regrets.

The written word cannot capture what has changed for me. The pain, the despair, the grief, and agony of my old life is an old story that is no longer relevant. Shiloh brought me to God and showed me that God is not an impersonal judge but a loving eternal friend and benefactor.

Recently, I discovered and listened to a short series of voice messages from the first year of my acquaintance with

Shiloh. In them, Shiloh explained clearly and concisely a basic concept about how God brings us what we need to see about ourselves. As though from a great distance, I heard a woman completely missing his main point. I could see how tightly she clung to her own ideas. I could see with great clarity how a defensive wall conspired to plug her ears to his words. I could hear how skilled he was, in repeating the concept in different ways from different angles using examples from her own life. Then I could hear when she finally understood, how thrilled she was to see this new way of looking at life.

That woman was me. But she is so far removed from who I am now, that I do not recognize myself in her. I was stunned to hear how invested I was in my views. I saw how I clung to my way of seeing things and that this blocked my understanding of all that Shiloh said. Such was the power of my mis-trained mind, I could not see the simple truth of his words. Only my fervent desire to be released from the misery of my life and the feeling that I could trust him, got me through those first months when I had not a single clue of my misperceptions nor any idea of who he was and what he could show me.

I marvel at how Shiloh was able to dissolve the boundaries I had erected to protect myself from others. His presence and skill healed deep psychological wounds and allowed me to open my heart to God.

I pondered the completed manuscript of this book and a surprising feeling arose. Terror. As I examined this massive fear, the reason showed itself quite clearly—a deeply rooted belief that to speak of myself was selfish.

This was the dark line that Shiloh had seen inside me, the one that said I was unworthy even of speaking. It was the reason I had not spoken up about the abuse I endured and set the stage for many troubles in my adult life. The idea that my feelings were irrelevant and unwanted eventually led to partnerships and relationships with people who did not value me. It likely was the source of the long delay in finishing this testimony.

I cried for a long while, releasing the idea of being unworthy that had been laid upon me when I was too young to know differently. I accepted my parents for their lack of skill in modeling how to value feelings. They each had suffered greatly; their pain was passed to me and my siblings unintentionally.

I told Shiloh of the massive release and he said, "That is a beautiful realization. You can see that if you had not experienced this trauma, you would not be where you are now."

"God bless my mother for all she did for me," I replied fervently. I knew Shiloh was right. I would never have sought the truth of myself and the truth of God if I had not been so bruised from life. What a huge favor she did me, as did all those who I thought treated me badly. Partners, friends, brother—all doing me their soul's favor of turning me to the One who would never judge me, who would always be there for me, and whose Love is perfect and eternal.

That night, I had a dream that I was lying in a rowboat with my eyes closed. A huge eagle flew to my side and sat next to me, bumping me over and over with its head until I opened my eyes. Then, it opened its huge beak and leaned over my face and I could see inside its mouth. The golden eagle placed its beak over my nose and breathed into my lungs.

One evening, as Shiloh and I spoke on the phone, before my eyes appeared something quite unusual.

Shiloh stood in front of me. But he was made almost entirely of flames. He seemed immense and I looked up at him, confused and awed by the fire that did not consume him.

Then he held out his hands to me. I hesitated only for a moment before gripping them. I knew those flames would burn but I willingly chose the fire. Because the flame of truth that Shiloh bears burns away all fear, all misperception, and all pain, leaving only Love.

EPILOGUE

Just before this book went to press, two remarkable things happened.

As I prepared to leave my temporary accommodation in Scotland, I noticed a Bible on the bookshelf near the bed. Although I am not religious and haven't read the Bible in at least thirty years, I felt the urge to read through the gospels.

Late into the night, I read the accounts of Jesus' life in the gospels of Matthew and Mark. The next morning I resolved to finish reading the gospels but when I arrived at Luke 9:35-36, I stopped. Over and over, I read the words God spoke about Jesus on the mountaintop with Moses and Elijah at his side. It was like reading them for the first time.

"THIS IS MY SON, MY CHOSEN; LISTEN TO HIM."

In a sudden flash of great light, I saw the parallel to the exact words that I heard from God on the beach two years earlier. The structure and even the content were strikingly similar.

"I HAVE CHOSEN SHILOH;
YOU ARE NOT TO QUESTION HIM."

I had always known the message God delivered that day was not only for me. God asked me to tell everyone that we are to listen carefully, without reservations, to His chosen one, Shiloh.

That night I had a dream. I saw Shiloh in front of me and on his forehead was a red letter from the Hebrew alphabet, the *chet*. As I stared at this letter, ח, on his forehead, I heard a booming voice say,

"HE IS THE DOORWAY."